Puzzles, Games, and Tricks

Understanding the Mystery and Magic of Numbers

Jerome S. Meyer

Skyhorse Publishing

First published in 1961 as *Fun with Mathematics* by Premier Books, Fawcett Publications, Inc., Greenwich, Connecticut

First Skyhorse Publishing Edition 2017

Skyhorse Publishing books may be purchased in bulk at special discounts for sales promotion, corporate gifts, fund-raising, or educational purposes. Special editions can also be created to specifications. For details, contact the Special Sales Department, Skyhorse Publishing, 307 West 36th Street, 11th Floor, New York, NY 10018 or info@skyhorsepublishing.com.

Skyhorse® and Skyhorse Publishing® are registered trademarks of Skyhorse Publishing, Inc.®, a Delaware corporation.

Visit our website at www.skyhorsepublishing.com.

10 9 8 7 6 5 4 3 2 1

Library of Congress Cataloging-in-Publication Data is available on file.

Cover artwork: iStockphoto

Print ISBN: 978-1-5107-2780-9
Ebook ISBN: 978-1-5107-2781-6

Printed in the United States of America

To

All Young People

Who Love Mathematics

CONTENTS

CONTENTS

PREFACE

In writing *Fun with Mathematics* I have tried to include a great deal of new material that would interest everyone for whom mathematics has an appeal. The section on "More and More of Less and Less" gives in everyday common experience the fundamental principles of differential and integral calculus. The section on π, i and e explains the mystery and fascination of the imaginary numbers, and gives the derivation and application of logarithms in language that any freshman in high school can readily understand. As far as I know, the method of making a good slide rule from an ordinary ruler has never been published before, nor has the chart ever appeared in a book which instantly solves problems of the right triangle without the necessity of knowing any trigonometry. In the section on "Mathematical How-to-do's" you will learn how to divide a circle into any number of equal parts, how to enlarge or reduce a picture, how to make a sundial and shadow stick that will tell the time and date anywhere, and many other how-to-do's.

You don't need a knowledge of mathematics to enjoy this book, but if you have a smattering of elementary mathematics you will enjoy it all the more. Of special interest to the trickster is the section by Royal Heath on magic squares that work upside down and in the mirror as well as right side up. Here you will find many tricks and stunts based on mathematical principles.

In conclusion I want to thank Dr. Jekuthiel Ginsburg of Yeshiva University for permission to reprint some of the curiosa which appeared in *Scripta Mathematica;* Mr. Aaron Bakst for permission to use his method of deriving logarithms quickly as given in his book *Mathematics, Its Magic and Mastery* (published by Van Nostrand); to E. P. Dutton and Company, Crown Publishers and Greenberg: Publisher for permission to reprint some of the problems in my books *Fun-to-Do, Puzzle Paradise,* and *Fun for the Family;* and to Royal V. Heath for his fascinating section on The Magic of Numbers. My sincere thanks also to Dr. John Storck and Stephen W. Leibholz for their valuable assistance in editing and correcting this book.

JEROME S. MEYER

Puzzles, Games, and Tricks

THE WORLD OF NUMBERS

EXPLORING BOTH ENDS OF OUR NUMBER SYSTEM

WE ORDINARY mortals live in a world of numbers just about halfway between the inconceivably large and the incredibly small. The numbers in our lives range between several million in the upper limit to about 1/10000 in the lower limit, and in the daily personal lives of most of us numbers greater than a few thousand or smaller than a sixteenth of an inch seldom appear.

When numbers get into the hundreds of millions or billions they have no meaning for us. We read of the population of the United States being 150,000,000 but can't possibly conceive such a large number, and numbers like the money for defense or the total national debt—running into the hundreds of billions—make us yawn and say "Well, well." Of course if you are a banker or the owner of a high-circulation magazine, numbers in the millions don't faze you; if you are a highly skilled mechanic working in an airplane factory a ten-thousandth of an inch reading on a micrometer is nothing unusual. But who ever hears of a *trillion* or *quadrillion* or *sextillion* or an *octo-vigintillionth of a gram* in ordinary conversation? These terms, outlandish and impractical as they seem to us, belong to the scientist who not only "eats them for breakfast" but uses them to produce the thousands of scientific miracles that make our lives comfortable and our living standards the highest in the world.

To the astronomer a number like 5,000,000,000,000,000,000 miles is all in a day's work. It represents the distance in miles of a certain nebula or star cluster from the earth. It is 5 quintillion miles or somewhat less than one million light years. A light year is the distance that light, traveling at 186,000 miles per second, will travel in a year. To the atomic physicist a single gram contains about 1,000,000,000,000,000,000,000,000 electrons. This is more electrons than there are drops of water in the Atlantic and Pacific Oceans combined! Yes, unlike you and me, these scientists live in a world of numbers far beyond our comprehension, and they are continually playing with the very great or the very small.

Of course they don't write these giants or pigmies out in ciphers: that would be a waste of time and space. They merely represent them in powers of 10. The exponent tells the number of ciphers, so when you see 10^{24} you know that it means 1 with 24 zeroes after the 1. When you see 10^{-18} you know that it is a fraction with 1 in the numerator and 1 followed by 18 zeros in the denominator:

$$\frac{1}{1,000,000,000,000,000,000}$$

When the physicist speaks of the mass of the earth being 5.9×10^{27} grams he saves himself from writing 5,900,000,000,000,000,-000,000,000,000 grams. When he tells us that the energy locked up in a pound of matter is 4×10^{23} ergs he can't be bothered to write 400,000,000,000,000,000,000,000. We shall meet numbers in this section that are of this amazingly large or small order, so we might as well get used to the mathematical way of writing them.

NUMBER GIANTS–HOW MUCH IS A BILLION?

Suppose you had a billion dollars and, in your desire to be entirely unique, you decided to invest it, without interest or dividends, in a very bad stock company. Now suppose the corporation was so poorly run that it succeeded in losing a thousand dollars of your money every day in the week and still managed to stay in business. It would take more than two thousand years for you to lose that billion dollars!

Again assuming that you are seventeen years old and started now to count up to a billion, one count every second, day and night without stopping to eat or sleep. Of course you couldn't do this without going on shifts, so we'll assume that two of your seventeen-year-old friends help you out. By the time you reached a billion you would be in your late forties.

If your fountain pen were enlarged one billion times it would be 95,000 miles long and 8,000 miles high. The cap of your pen would be big enough to enclose the earth, whose diameter is roughly 7,900 miles. But a billion is only 10^9 and that is a mere nothing compared to the real giants. Suppose it were possible to tear a sheet of paper of a certain size and of about the thickness of this page, in half; and then to tear the pieces again in half, and then again in half, and to keep this up for fifty tearings. Each time you would be doubling the number of sheets of paper. The question is: How high a pile would fifty tearings make, and how big a sheet would you need to begin with, to get final sheets of about the size of this page? The answer is incredible but it can be easily verified. It is 2 raised to the 50th power and turns out to be 1,125,899,906,842,624 sheets of paper. Since each sheet would measure about one third of a square foot, this comes to 375,299,968,947,541 square feet or over 13,000,000 square miles, or a little less than one quarter the land area of the entire earth. Figuring 400 of these sheets to the inch, we would have a pile about 2,860,000,000,000 inches high. Divide this by 12 and we get about 230,000,000,000 feet. Now one million feet come to approximately 190 miles, so the pile would be more than 38,000,000 miles high!

Then there is the story of the ancient king who, being under obligation to one of his subjects, offered to reward him in any way he desired. The subject, a man of mathematical mind and modest tastes, simply asked for a chess board with one grain of wheat on the first square, two on the second, four on the third and so on, doubling the grains each time until all the squares on the board were accounted for. The old king was delighted and relieved with this simple request but was soon sorry that he granted it. To account for every square on the board in this fashion the king had to supply $2^{63} + 1$ grains of wheat which, in round numbers, is 9,460,000,000,000,000,000. Now, assuming that there are 250 grains in a cubic inch and 2,150 cubic inches in a bushel, one bushel will contain about 540,000 grains of wheat. This number, then, would amount to 17,382,000,000,000 bushels. Since the yearly output of wheat of the entire United States is a little more than 1 billion bushels it would take this nation 16,000 years to satisfy this "modest" subject of the king. The story goes no further but the chances are the king lost his temper and the subject lost his head long before the 64th square of the chess board was reached.

Now let us consider a real giant. Let us roughly try to determine the number of molecules of water on the surface of the earth. Of course such a problem is highly impractical and ridiculous but it will serve to show what a real giant looks like. Taking the area of the water on the earth as 140,000,000 square miles and the average depth of the oceans as 2 miles we have a total volume of water of about 280,000,000 cubic miles or, in other words, 2.8×10^8. Now there are 2.6×10^{10} square centimeters in a square mile and 1.6×10^5 centimeters to a mile. Therefore there are 4.1×10^{15} cubic centimeters in a cubic mile. Multiplying this by 2.8×10^8 we get 11.5×10^{23} or 1.15×10^{24} cubic centimeters of water on the face of the earth. It has been quite accurately calculated that there are 27×10^{18} molecules of water to the cubic centimeter so we conclude that the water molecules on this earth amount to approximately $(1.15 \times 10^{24}) \times (2.7 \times 10^{19}) = 3.1 \times 10^{43}$. This is otherwise known as 31 million, billion, billion, billion, billion molecules. Written out it looks like this: 31,000,000,000,000,000,-000,000,000,000,000,000,000,000,000.

A staggering number is the mass of the sun in grams, which turns out to be 19 with 32 ciphers after it, or 19×10^{32}. Of course this is completely incomprehensible and inconceivable, but it still is a dwarf when multiplied by the number of molecules of hydrogen in a gram which is 27×10^{18}. We can then say that the approximate number of molecules of hydrogen which make up the mass of the sun is 510×10^{50}. If this number seems large to you, consider Eddington's estimate of the number of electrons in the universe. This turns out to be about 157×10^{77} which according to Eddington, who figured it out, is: 15,747,724,136,275,002,577,-605,653,961,181,555,468,044,717,914,527,116,709,366,231,425,-076,185,631,031,296.

Now we come to a giant of giants, a number that is so ridiculously large that it never could apply to anything. Oddly enough it can be written with three nines and is represented by 9^{9^9}. This is 9 multiplied by itself 387,420,489 times. Written in numerals the size we are using, the number would stretch for a thousand miles. To read it normally would take more than a week. What it is nobody knows although it does begin with 428,124,-773 . . . and ends with 89. That number of bacteria would overflow the Milky Way. The number of snowflakes that have fallen since the earth began does not even approach this giant. It is more than 4 million times as large as the number of electrons in the universe, which we just discussed.

INFINITY

ANOTHER EXTREMELY important idea in mathematics is infinity. Any quantity that increases without ever stopping will ultimately become and remain greater than any definite number we can name. It will then be infinite. Of course infinity and the infinite are vital terms and concepts in higher mathematics. We have briefly touched on this subject in the section called *More and More of Less and Less*. The theory of limits and infinite series gives us among other things the trigonometric tables and tables of logarithms.

An excellent example of one practical application of infinity is

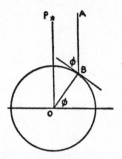

FIGURE I

an elementary principle in navigation. Astronomers and navigators consider that the earth is in the center of a celestial sphere commonly called the heavens. The radius of this sphere—the distance from the earth to the imaginary sphere itself—is infinity. The captain of a ship in midocean takes his sextant and sights on the north star (Polaris).

In the diagram, Figure 1, the circle represents the earth. The line OB makes an angle ϕ with the equator and this angle is of course the latitude of the point B. A tangent to the circle at B represents the horizon at latitude B. Now our captain sights on the north star P, which is almost directly above the north pole of the earth. If the radius of the celestial sphere were not considered as infinite the line of sight from B would meet the North Star P in the diagram. But because the radius is infinite, BA becomes parallel to OP. It follows then that the angle AB makes with the line OA is equal to the angle ϕ or the latitude. Our captain can then tell his latitude merely by the angle that Polaris makes with the horizon.

MUCH ADO ABOUT NOTHING

IN CONVERSATION "nothing" is a word like any other word and as such can easily be confused with "something." The old riddle,

"Which would you rather have, complete happiness in life or a ham sandwich?" is a good illustration. The answer is, "A ham sandwich. Nothing is better than complete happiness in life, and a ham sandwich is better than nothing." Here we use nothing as a definite something and, of course, the comparison is ridiculous. In the same way we prove that a cow has nine legs by saying that no cow has five legs and *a* cow has four legs more than no cow.

The mathematician does not stand for this sort of nonsense. While a layman like Willie's father may be puzzled and annoyed by the following question, the mathematician has a logical and complete answer for it:

"If I add nothing to 5 I don't add anything so I don't change its value. The same holds true when I take nothing away from 5. Now if I multiply 5 by nothing I don't multiply it by anything and, of course, I leave it alone and its value is not changed. Now I know that 5 times nothing is nothing but I'm sure that it should be 5. Why isn't any number times nothing equal to that number for the reason I have just given?"

Willie's father could not answer him satisfactorily. If he had been up in his mathematics he would explain the difference in meaning between the English word "nothing" and the mathematical term "zero."

The simplest way to answer Willie's dilemma is to show that multiplication is really repeated addition. Multiplying 5 by 3 is the same as adding *two* 5's to the original 5, thus: $5 + 5 + 5$. In the same way 5×2 is the same as adding *one* 5 to itself, thus: $5 + 5$; 5 times 1 is the same as adding *no* 5's to the original 5. The number of times we add the number to itself is always *one less* than the number we multiply by; so, in general, multiplying a number A by another number B is just the same as adding A to itself $B-1$ *times*. In multiplying 5 by zero we add 5 to itself $0 - 1$ times or, in other words, we add -5 to the original 5 and the result is zero.

Another and more complete mathematical way to explain Willie's problem is this: Instead of calling zero "nothing," let us call it a fraction with some numerator, say 1, whose denominator is larger than any number we can name. The fraction 1 divided by 100 quintillion is so small that for all practical purposes it could be called zero. If we make the denominator still larger such as 100 octillion, the fraction is well on its way toward the vanishing point or zero. Now you can readily see that 5 times this inconceivably small fraction will make no difference at all. It will still be, for all practical purposes, equal to zero. Reasoning in this way you can see that when the denominator of a fraction becomes and remains larger than any number that can be named—becomes infinite, in other words—the value of the fraction will become equal to zero and any number in the numerator, no matter what, cannot keep that fraction from equaling zero, hence zero times any number is always zero.

Of course you must have observed from this that as the denominator of a fraction approaches infinity (written ∞) the value of the fraction approaches zero. We can then say that zero equals $\frac{1}{\infty}$.

Now we can see why any number to the zero power equals 1. Let the number be A. Raising A to the zero power, from what we have just said, is the same as taking the infinite root of A or

$$A^\circ = A^{\frac{1}{\infty}} = \sqrt[\infty]{A}$$

We can show that the infinite root of any number is equal to 1 regardless of the size of the number. Take 64 for example:

$$
\begin{aligned}
\text{The square root} &= \sqrt[2]{64} = 8.00000 \\
\text{The cube root} &= \sqrt[3]{64} = 4.00000 \\
\text{The 4th root} &= \sqrt[4]{64} = 2.8284 \ldots \\
\text{The 10th root} &= \sqrt[10]{64} = 1.5156 \ldots \\
\text{The 100th root} &= \sqrt[100]{64} = 1.0425 \ldots \\
\text{The 1000th root} &= \sqrt[1000]{64} = 1.0069 \ldots \\
\text{The 10,000th root} &= \sqrt[10,000]{64} = 1.0004 \ldots \\
& \cdots\cdots\cdots\cdots\cdots \\
\text{The infinite root} &= \sqrt[\infty]{64} = 1.00000 \\
\text{That is,} \quad 64^\circ &= 1
\end{aligned}
$$

THE WORLD OF NUMBERS

You can see that the infinite root or zero power of any positive number will behave in the same way and ultimately be equal to 1.

Zero and infinity are two of the most important concepts in all mathematics. The calculus, or the study of the ratio of two infinitesimals, gives us the instantaneous rate of change of one variable with respect to the other. In doing so it becomes one of the most vital tools in science.

Most people use the word infinitesimal in the wrong sense. You cannot have an infinitesimal quantity of a thing because the definition of the word is a quantity becoming smaller than any fixed number we can think of, no matter how small. Strangely enough, the limiting ratio of two infinitesimals is *not* always zero divided by zero but, instead, an exact value. If an automobile travels 60 miles in one hour would you say that that car traveled at the rate of 60 miles an hour? Of course not. It might have stopped somewhere along the line and made up time later on. We can only say that its *average speed* is 60 miles an hour. If now we cut down the distance and the time to a mile a minute (the same ratio) we give it less chance to average and the velocity of the car becomes more exact. We can keep doing this as much as we please. It travels 88 feet per second and here the velocity is much more exact. It follows from this that as the distance and time get smaller and smaller and approach zero as a limit, their ultimate ratio (distance divided by time) is the exact value or instantaneous rate of 60 miles an hour. This instantaneous rate at any given instant is of the utmost importance in higher mathematics and science.

One of the best ways to appreciate zero is to consider permutations and chance. The number of ways three objects can be arranged, for example, is $1 \times 2 \times 3$ which in mathematical terms is called factorial 3 and written 3! This is easily shown for *A, B* and *C* as follows:

$$ABC \quad BAC \quad CAB$$
$$ACB \quad BCA \quad CBA$$

If now we take on the letter D, we see that it can be placed first, second, third or fourth in each of the above six combinations. We then have 4×6 or 24 combinations. You can verify this for yourself by setting up four columns of six combinations each, the first column beginning with A, the second with B, the third with C and the fourth with D. So factorial 4 (4!) is $1 \times 2 \times 3 \times 4$, or 24.

In the same way the number of ways eight different objects can be arranged is factorial 8 (8!), or $1 \times 2 \times 3 \times 4 \times 5 \times .6 \times 7 \times 8$, or 40,320.

Now try to imagine the number of arrangements that can be made in a single pack of cards, using all the cards for each arrangement. This, of course, is 52! which turns out to be 1.06×10^{68}. This means that the chance of each bridge player getting 13 cards of the same suit in order of suits and rank from a shuffled pack in a single deal is 1 in 1.06×10^{68}. We can safely say that, for all practical purposes this is no chance at all or, in other words, that the chance is zero. If everybody in the world, men, women and children, played bridge night and day, dealing hands at the rate of 1 a minute, this particular situation would come up once in 10^{48} years. Since the entire solar system is not yet 4×10^{9} years old, the chance of each bridge player getting 13 cards of the same suit in proper order and suits can be safely put as "never." But you must remember that the reasoning applies to any specific collection of hands whatever, provided each hand is specified in detail as to the order in which the cards are dealt.

Of course this can go on and on. Think of the chance of ten bottles falling off a window sill, crashing to the sidewalk and smashing, each of them, into exactly the same number of pieces, of exactly the same shapes. If you extend this to 100 bottles you will readily see that you can arrive at zero, for all practical purposes.

MATHEMATICAL MIDGETS

THE COLLOIDAL chemist deals in extremely minute quantities. Colloidal particles are measured not in millimeters (a millimeter is about 1/25 of an inch) but in millionths of a millimeter, called millimicrons, and designated by the symbol μ. A millimicron is about 1/25 millionth of an inch, so you can see how small colloidal particles are. But colloidal particles are enormous when compared with molecules. Molecules are so small that ten million of them would fit on the head of a pin with plenty of room to spare. If every molecule in a quart of water were the size of a grain of sand there would be enough sand to make a desert the size of the Sahara. F. W. Aston, the British scientist, estimated that if you were able to pour a million molecules of water into a milk bottle every second and you kept at it day and night without ever stopping, it would take more than one hundred million years to fill the bottle.

Of course molecules are invisible, even under the most powerful light microscope, but even they are *enormous* when compared with the nucleus of the atom! The hydrogen atom is less than one thousandth the size of a molecule. You can realize that that is pretty minute, but the atom is mostly empty space. The nucleus of the atom, the main mass of it, is one trillionth the size of the atom (this is one million-millionth the size of the atom, which in turn is about one thousandth the size of a molecule). Since there are approximately twenty-seven million, million, million molecules in a gram, which in turn is 1/28 of an ounce, you can get a slight idea of how small the nucleus of an atom is. An electron is even smaller than the nucleus of the atom. The electron is the smallest thing we know, and is considered generally to have very close to zero mass.

So you can see that these incomprehensible giants and midgets approaching infinity in one direction and zero in the other are the toys of the scientist. They are not of much use to the layman and certainly far beyond his comprehension, but he takes advantage of the motion of quintillions of billions of electrons every time he turns on his radio or his television set or, in fact, whenever he makes use of any electrical device.

MORE AND MORE OF LESS AND LESS

IF A millionaire offered you your choice between a barrel filled with half dollars and the same barrel filled with dimes, which

FIGURE 2

would you choose? If you chose the barrel of half dollars because you thought it would be worth more than the barrel of dimes, you would be wrong. The dimes, being very much smaller and thinner than the half dollars, would fill the barrel more completely and there would be much less space between the coins. By actual count there will be about six times as many dimes as half dollars in the barrel, or about 20% more in money value.

In the same way, if there were such a coin as a silver penny it would be very small, probably the size of a buckshot, and the same barrel filled with these tiny coins would be worth much more than either the dimes or the half dollars because they would fill the barrel so much more completely. But there would be tiny spaces between these minute coins, so if we kept on reducing the size of the silver pieces and increasing their number, we would approach the maximum value of silver in the barrel. When we finally had trillions of billions of invisible particles of silver, each the size of a silver atom, we would have the maximum value in the barrel; this takes place only when the barrel has become a solid chunk of silver.

The more and more we have of less and less the nearer we come to an ultimate maximum. This is strikingly shown in Figure 3. Here we start with a photograph which is fairly indistinct because

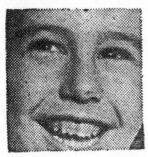 

FIGURE 3

it has been chopped up by a screen. There are about 60 lines to the inch and you can almost count the tiny dots and squares in the picture. Now look at the next picture. Everything gets clearer and clearer. This is because the screen through which it is taken is finer and finer and the number of dots and squares in the picture is smaller and smaller—and there are more and more of them. Obviously the more we have of these tiny dots and the smaller the dots are, the more exact will be the picture they form and only when they are molecular in size and there are many billions of them (a screenless photograph) would we ultimately have a picture which is exact. Here again we have more and more of less and less.

Now bear in mind that in each of these examples the relationships do not change. The barrels are the same size and the picture represents the same scene in each case. This is important, as we shall see later on.

We might continue our reasoning further and say that there

should be still another point at which each tiny speck vanishes to zero and there are an infinite number of them. Would not this point be even more exact? Doesn't true accuracy and exactness, according to what we have said, result from an infinite quantity of nothing at all? Offhand it would certainly seem so. If we increase the number of sides of a regular polygon, each side grows smaller in length and the polygon will ultimately turn into the circumference of a circle. It would seem that a circle is really a regular polygon of an infinite number of sides, each side of which

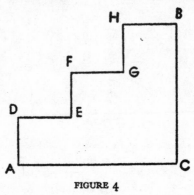

FIGURE 4

is zero in length. Of course this isn't so. An infinite quantity of nothing is meaningless since it has no definite value. A tiny angle of one second in the center of the earth would subtend an arc of only 100 feet on the earth's surface. To appreciate how near this arc comes to being a straight line, think of a lake only 100 feet wide where the water is absolutely still like a large mirror. For all practical purposes the surface of this lake is absolutely flat. Yet we know that it is still an arc and consequently it must be curved, even though the curvature is negligible. As a matter of fact, the surface of the lake at the center would be less than 1/100 of an inch higher than it is at the edge—just enough to keep the lake surface from being absolutely flat. In other words this is a side of a regular polygon of 1,296,000 sides and the difference between each side and the surface of the earth is less than a hundredth of an inch, yet that difference is there and will never vanish. So infinity times zero must be ruled out of mathematical reasoning. The fallacy involved in this operation is beautifully shown in Figures 4 to 7.

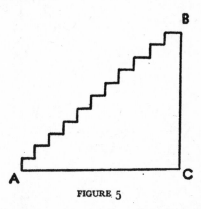

FIGURE 5

In Figure 4 the distance from *A* to *C* is obviously the sum of the three horizontal distances *DE*, *FG*, and *HB* and the vertical distance from *C* to *B* is the sum of the vertical distances *AD*, *EF*, and *GH*. Now look at Figure 5 and you will see that there are eleven steps, yet the sum of all the horizontal treads equals *AC* and the sum of all the vertical risers equals *CB*. We can continue this process indefinitely, making more and more steps, each step being smaller and smaller as shown in Figure 6 and still the sum of all the horizontals equals line *AC* and the sum of all the verticals equals line *CB*. In Figure 7 there are so many tiny steps that they require a magnifying glass to see them. The line *AB* appears to be a perfectly straight line until you examine it with a magnifying glass and see that it is made up of about 160 tiny steps, the sum of whose sides equals the side *AC* plus the side *CB*. Does this mean that ultimately all the millions and billions of invisible steps from *A* to *B* will actually form a straight line? It would seem so, just as we say that a regular polygon of billions and trillions of sides will ultimately become a circumference. But if this is true, then we have the great difficulty of the hypotenuse of a right triangle

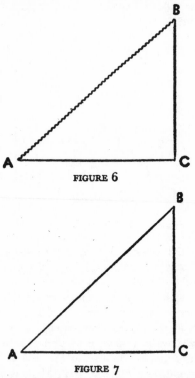

FIGURE 6

FIGURE 7

being equal to the sum of its other two sides; this, of course, is utter nonsense. The truth of the matter is that these steps, in increasing in number and decreasing in size, *approach* the straight line *AB* but never actually become a straight line. We might have ten quadrillion of the steps and could not possibly distinguish them from the straight line *AB* even with a high-power microscope, yet we know that they do not form the straight line *AB* since the sum of all their verticals and the sum of all their horizontals still equals *AC* plus *CB*.

And so we see that as we keep on taking more and more and more of less and less and less, we get nearer and nearer to a limit but never numerically reach it; yet, in that vitally important and fascinating branch of mathematics known as the calculus, we continually speak of "the limiting value" and "in the limit such and such will be true." How do we get around the fact that these variables *approach* but never numerically *reach* the limit? How for instance do we have the right to say that 2 is the limit of the continuous series

$$1 + \frac{1}{2} + \frac{1}{4} + \frac{1}{8} + \frac{1}{16} = \frac{1}{2^a}$$

We might carry this out to 30 terms and we would still have

$$1 + \frac{1073741823}{1073741824}$$

which would be .0000000001 less than 2, but *still would not be* 2. We get over this difficulty by saying that the limit of any variable is reached when the difference between that variable and its limit becomes and remains less in numerical value than any positive number that it is possible to name. The variable gets closer and closer to the limiting value, and stays close to it. In fact, the difference between the limit and the variable becomes smaller than any number we can name, no matter how small this difference number is. You can name a positive number less than .0000000001 in the above example, and hence the limit 2 has not been reached. We don't ever and can't ever specify that number since it is smaller than any number we can name, yet *it is not zero*. To make this a little clearer let us take the line *AB*:

A   *B*

We know very well that we can keep on dividing this line in half and we shall always have a half remaining. As we do this we approach A or B as the case may be, but never numerically reach it. We do reach it theoretically when the difference between the last division and the point A (or B) becomes and remains less than any positive number we can think of. This saves the situation and keeps us from dividing by zero, which is ruled out of mathematical reasoning. If dividing by zero were allowed, any number would equal any other number, as you can see from the following:

$$
\begin{aligned}
&\text{Let} && b = a \\
&\text{Then} && ab = a^2 \\
&\text{And} && ab - b^2 = a^2 - b^2 \\
&\text{Then} && b(a - b) = (a + b)(a - b) \\
&\text{Dividing by } (a - b), && b = b + a \\
&\text{Or, if } a = 1, && 1 = 2
\end{aligned}
$$

This result, of course, is absurd. We always *approach* zero and *approach* infinity and ultimately arrive at a point where the difference from them becomes and remains less than any positive number possible to name. In this way we avoid "an infinite amount of nothing," which is meaningless and would make the hypotenuse of a right triangle equal to the sum of its other two sides. And we also avoid division by zero which is also meaningless and makes 1 equal to 2 or any other number. Now let us take a few examples from the calculus to see how this principle is applied.

. By means of the calculus we can figure the exact area of any irregular closed curve. This is done by summing up an inconceivably large number of inconceivably narrow rectangles or tri-. angles. In the days before the calculus only approximate areas were obtainable. Mathematicians would divide the diagram into equal strips as shown in Figure 8. Each strip was a rectangle whose area was easy to find and the sum total of the areas of all these rectangles was "more or less" the area of the irregular figure. Now you can see from the figures there are always some areas, small as they are, that are not accounted for. In the figures these are blackened in.

As the width of each of these strips is decreased we naturally get more strips or rectangles, and as they get smaller and smaller in width there are more and more of them, filling out the irregular area more completely. We conclude then that the area of this irregular diagram is the sum of the areas of all these rectangles as their widths approach zero as a limit. In such a condition there

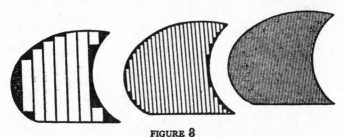

FIGURE 8

would be no leftover areas and the entire space would be accounted for. Only by means of the calculus are we able to sum up this inconceivably large quantity of infinitesimal areas to find the exact area of the irregular diagram.

This summing up is not strictly an addition process. Unlike the ancients, who added the areas of all the rectangles together, the process of integration employs a different method, and is therefore able to sum up this inconceivably large number of rectangles whose widths are incredibly small. Note again that the bases of the rectangles never equal zero, since their areas would then vanish. They come nearer to zero than any number possible to name.

Perhaps one of the causes for misunderstanding in the study of the calculus, particularly for beginners, is reconciling the approaching of a limit with the limit itself. The beginner will naturally think, for example, that the circle is a regular polygon of an infinite number of sides, each side having no length at all. We have already shown that as the number of sides of a regular polygon approaches infinity, each side approaching zero in length, there will come a time or a point at which the difference between the polygon and the circumference of an inscribed circle will be less than any number no matter how small.

Infinity and zero can never be reached by any process of addition or division; they can only be approached. You can divide

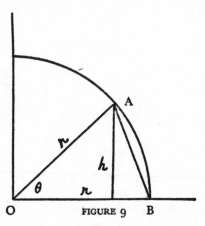

FIGURE 9

a line in half from now until doomsday and you will still have a half to divide; you will never get to zero. You can double a quantity from now until doomsday, yet the difference between your last valuation and infinity will still be infinite.

One of the best-known formulas in mathematics is πr^2, or the formula for the area of a circle. Everybody knows this formula but not many know how it is derived.

Figure 9 shows a portion of a circle in which we have the triangle OAB. From elementary geometry we know that the area of this triangle is half the base times the altitude or

$$\text{area of } \triangle OAB = \tfrac{1}{2}OB \times h$$

But OB = radius = r, $\therefore$ area of $\triangle OAB = \tfrac{1}{2}rh$. But $h \doteq r \sin \theta$, $\therefore$ area of $\triangle OAB = \tfrac{1}{2}r^2 \sin \theta$. Now, as θ gets smaller and smaller the sine of θ becomes ever more nearly equal to the angle θ

itself (in radian measurement). From what we have been discussing you can see that when θ becomes, and remains, less than any value we can name, $\sin \theta = \theta$ and the area of this inconceivably narrow triangle is $\frac{1}{2}r^2\theta$.

In the section on π, i and e we shall see that $360° = 2\pi$. Summing up the inconceivably large number of these inconceivably small triangles which make up the area of the circle, we get $\theta = 360°$ or 2π, and the area of the circle is

$$\frac{1}{2}r^2\theta \text{ when } \theta = 2\pi, \text{ or } \frac{1}{2}(2\pi r^2) = \pi r^2$$

NUMBER SYSTEMS
OTHER THAN OURS

HOW DID THE ROMANS MULTIPLY AND DIVIDE?

HERE ARE some simple problems in Roman mathematics. Can you solve them without translating the Roman symbols into the numbers we use?

Multiply MCCVII by LXXIV	Add: LXVII
	CMIX
Divide MCMLXVIII by XCI	·MCMII
	VIII

Certainly if you bear in mind that "MCCVII is 1207 and LXXIV is 74," you will have no difficulty whatever, but how to work with all these M's and C's and L's and X's is another matter. How did the Romans manage to manipulate these strange symbols and come out all right? Did a Roman grocer in the ancient equivalent for a supermarket, actually add such Roman numbers on papyrus and give the correct change for a gold *aureus*? Imagine what a time you would have working out your income tax in Roman numbers! And what did the Roman engineers do? How did they know, for example, that the square root of LXIV is VIII? By what possible method could they calculate?

As far as we know the Romans did all their calculating on a device known as an abacus, resembling a child's toy and shown in Figure 10. They used this abacus as quickly and efficiently as we use an adding machine, or an engineer a slide rule. Just as

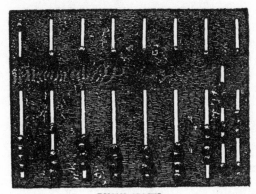

ROMAN ABACUS

FIGURE 10

there is practically no paper and pencil addition today in our banks and business houses because of adding and other machines, so there was practically no written work in arithmetic in the days of Ancient Rome because of the abacus.

Before discussing the abacus and how it works it is extremely interesting to see how the Roman numerals got that way. Of

FIGURE 11

course the I and II and III are obvious since they represent one, two, and three objects respectively, but the five, ten, fifty, one hundred, and one thousand, which the Romans represented by V, X, L, C and M are not quite so obvious. The X for 10 is explained in two ways. One explanation says that it represents both hands showing the 10 fingers (note that the word *digits* means fingers as well as numbers), as given in Figure 11. This takes the form of X and, of course, half of this or 5 is V. The other explanation says that the Romans made marks just as we do today when we tally something. We make vertical strokes and strike out every five as in Figure 12, and so on, so we can count the groups

FIGURE 12   FIGURE 13

and multiply by 5. The Romans made 9 vertical strokes and crossed them out as in Figure 13, and hence the cross became the symbol for 10 and half of it became the symbol for 5. The L is from a corrupted form of the Greek letter used previously to denote 50 and the C is from the Latin *centum* meaning 100.

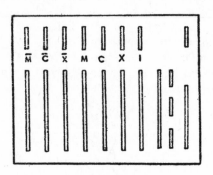

FIGURE 14

The M comes from the Latin *mille*, which is 1000. The word *mile* is directly derived from this word because the Roman pace was 2 steps of $2\frac{1}{2}$ feet, or 5 feet—from the heel of one foot to that same heel when it next touched the ground—and *mille passus* was 1000 paces or 5000 feet.

A letter repeated once or twice represents double or treble its value: XX is 20 and XXX is 30. A letter placed before another letter of greater value decreases the greater value by the amount of the letter value: XL is 40, or 10 from 50; IV is 4 or 1 from 5; XC is 90 or 10 from 100. The opposite applies to letters which follow one of greater value; they add to its value by the amount of the letter: LX is 60 or 50 + 10; LXX is 70 or 50 + 20. A line placed over a letter multiplies that letter by 1000: $\overline{X}$ is 10,000; $\overline{C}$ is 100,000; $\overline{M}$ is 1,000,000. And so we have the Roman numeral system as follows:

Letter	Value	Letter	Value
I	1	LX	60
II	2	LXX	70
III	3	LXXX	80
IV	4	XC	90
V	5	C	100
VI	6	D	500
VII	7	M	1,000
VIII	8	$\overline{V}$	5,000
IX	9	$\overline{X}$	10,000
X	10	$\overline{L}$	50,000
XX	20	$\overline{C}$	100,000
XXX	30	$\overline{D}$	500,000
XL	40	$\overline{M}$	1,000,000
L	50		

The Roman abacus was a metal plate having a number of vertical grooves which carried stone buttons. Here we have another interesting derivation. The Latin word for pebble is *calculus*, from which we get *calculate*. To calculate, according to the Romans, was to manipulate these stones or pebbles on the abacus.

Figure 14 shows the grooved plate without the stones, while in Figure 15 the stones are in their grooves. Four stones are in each long groove and one stone in each short groove. Note the Roman numerals on the plate. Omitting, for the time being, the first three sets of grooves at the right, we have a unit groove I, a tens groove X, a hundreds groove C, a thousands groove M, a ten thousands groove $\overline{X}$, a hundred thousands groove $\overline{C}$ and a millions groove $\overline{M}$. The four stones at the bottom are 1, 2, 3 and

4 or their multiples of 10; the one stone above represents 5 or its multiple of 10, depending upon the groove it is in. The number 3 would show three stones moved up in the units groove; 30 would be three stones moved up in the tens groove; 300 the same

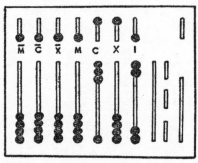

FIGURE 15

in the hundreds groove; and so on. In the same way 5, 50, 500, 5,000, etc., would be the single stone in a short groove moved up in the proper groove.

The grooves at the right are to handle fractions, and Figure 10 shows that there are five buttons below and one above. The fractions are on a duodecimal system, each button indicating 1/12 instead of 1/10 and the button in the short groove representing 6/12 instead of 5/10. One of the grooves for fractions is divided into three short grooves with the top button representing 1/24, the middle button 1/48 and the lower one 1/72.

So expert were the Romans on this abacus that they could add, multiply, divide and subtract whole numbers or fractions just as fast as we use adding machines.

In Figure 15 we can see an abacus set for 852; let us suppose we want to add 218 to this. Starting with the 8 in the unit column, we realize that the 8 and the 2 will give us an additional 1 in the 10 column, so we move all buttons back in the unit column and push one button up in the ten column. We now come to the 1 in 218 which must be added to the 1 we already pushed up in the 10 column hence our ten column now shows 7 instead of the previous 5 (Figure 16). Now looking at the hundreds place we

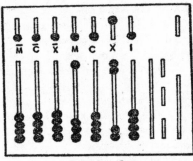

FIGURE 16

can see that the 8 and the 2 make 10 so we clear the hundreds completely and move one button up in the thousands.

The abacus has long since disappeared from our modern civilization (although it is still used in the Orient). Thanks to the Hindus and Arabs, our priceless system of numerals—those nine vitally important digits and zero—run our lives today. It is inconceivable how we could work without them; what our arithmetic and mathematics would be in the absence of the decimal system. To our common numerals we owe more than we realize of the comforts and luxuries that science has given us today. To the Arabs and Hindus we owe everlasting thanks for introducing these digits to us.

Our present numerals are usually referred to as Arabic, but they are really Hindu-Arabic and date back to the third century B.C. It is also likely that the Persians and Egyptians played an important part in developing these ten symbols and that the intercourse between the traders of that time brought these numbers from country to country and so, after many years, developed them into the symbols we now use.

In another section of this book we discuss Fibonacci numbers, named after the great mathematician who is also known as Leonardo of Pisa. His father made Leonardo learn the use of the abacus when a small boy and Leonardo developed an insatiable taste for mathematics. In his travels through Egypt, Syria and Greece he collected an abundance of material on Arabic numerals and in 1202 published his great work *Liber Abaci*, which was responsible for the adoption of the Arabic notation into western civilization. From that time on arithmetic and algebra flourished and expanded and paved the way for such geniuses as Descartes, Fermat, Pascal, Galileo, Newton, Euler, Maxwell and hundreds of others, who are immortalized by their enormous contributions to modern science and mathematics.

The perfecting of the so-called Arabic notation was due almost entirely to the Hindus, who were among the greatest thinkers and philosophers of their day. The nine numbers that we use today were born way back in the third century B.C., although in appearance they were entirely different then from what they are now. The zero came into our present number system much later, but the basic principles of the Hindu-Arabic numeral system were the very beginning of arithmetic and algebra.

Much later, in the tenth century, the processes of addition and subtraction began to take on more of their present-day appearance. The idea of the "carry-over" was invented and combined with the place system. Numbers were added by arranging their digits in columns. All unit digits were in the farthest right-hand column, all tens digits in the column next to the left, all hundreds digits to the left of the tens, and so on. The unit column was added and if the result came to more than ten it was split up, the unit figure was put down, and the ten figure "carried over in the mind" and added to the tens column. The same was true for all the other columns. Early twelfth-century addition showed digits struck out and the final result corrected thus:

```
59137
 6120
 3813
6̶5̶0̶6̶0
 9 7
```

In the place and carry-over system lies the difference between the Hindu-Arabic numbers and those used by the Greeks and Romans. Place has no settled meaning with Roman numbers: 1,000,000, for example, has seven places with us and only one with the Romans, since they represented it by $\overline{M}$; 38 has only two places with us and seven places in the Roman system—XXXVIII. In our system we can add up one column at a time and if it comes to 10 or more we just "carry-over" to the next column and thus have our own abacus on paper—and, incidentally, a much simpler one. Look at the identical example in Roman numerals and in ours:

C	100
M	1000
VIII	8
MCMXIII	1913
MMMXXI	3021

Early multiplication was simplified by resolving the problem into a series of steps in each of which one of the numbers was doubled while the other was halved (temporarily neglecting fractions), until the second number was reduced to unity. To multiply 23 × 17, for example, the early mathematicians doubled the 23 each time and cut the 17 in half thus:

23	46	92	184	368
17	8	4	2	1

They then added another 23 to the result (for the fraction neglected during halving), giving 391. This was exactly equivalent to multiplying 23 × 16 and adding one more 23 to the product, since 17 is one more than 16: 368, the last number on this line plus 23 equals 391 which is 17 × 23. If we had multiplied by 18 or 19 we should have to add 2 × 23 or 3 × 23 to 368 thus: 18 × 23 gives 368 + 46 = 414; 19 × 23 gives 368 + 69 = 437.

Some great and unheralded genius in the fourteenth or fifteenth century discovered the priceless value and vital importance of the multiplication tables. One of the early tables appears in Widman's *Arithmetic*, published in Leipzig in 1489 and shown in Figure 17.

FIGURE 17

Such tables, and the fact that they were made compulsory learning with every elementary school child so that he knows the multiplication tables as well as he knows the alphabet and will never forget them, is one of man's greatest achievements. Everyone, unless he is illiterate, knows his multiplication tables. They are just as important as reading and writing. It is difficult to imagine anyone who can read and write his own name not knowing how much 4 × 3 or 6 × 7 is.

And so the tables which have been drilled into school children for centuries, together with our place and "carry-over" system in addition and multiplication and the "borrow" system in subtraction and division, have given us the fundamentals of elementary arithmetic. Thanks to the genius of the Hindus and the Arabs of the twelfth and thirteenth centuries we have been able through elementary arithmetic to build up mathematics and discover the universe of science, unlocking thousands of nature's secrets for our convenience and comfort. Most of us take the ten digits and the four processes in arithmetic entirely for granted, never giving a thought to how they developed and how vitally important they are to you and me.

BABE RUTH HIT 111100 HOME RUNS IN ONE SEASON

No WONDER everyone in Peter's class laughs at him. He adds and multiplies in the queerest way, yet he always gets the correct results. Only the other day, when asked to add 14, 12 and 6, he went to the blackboard and wrote:

$$
\begin{array}{r}
1110 \\
1100 \\
110 \\
\hline
100000
\end{array}
$$

and announced the result as 32. Thinking that Peter was playing a trick on her, the teacher asked him to multiply 4 by 6. Peter in the same careless way wrote:

$$100 \times 110 = 11000$$

and announced the result as 24.

Of course the class had a lot of fun from all this foolishness, but the teacher didn't enjoy it so much. She ordered Peter to take down certain numbers and multiply them without any more showing off. But Peter was not showing off at all. He can handle the same problems as the rest of the class. When asked to multiply 41 by 57 he did it exactly as follows:

	41 ×	57
	20 ×	114
("I divide by 2	10 ×	228	("I multiply by 2
each time")	5 ×	456	each time")
	2 ×	912
	1 ×	1824

33

"Now, "said Peter, "when I get to 1 in the left-hand column, I cross out all even numbers on the left, along with their corresponding numbers on the right, and add what remains like this:

$$
\begin{array}{r}
41 \times \ \ 57 \\
5 \times \ \ 456 \\
1 \times \underline{1824} \\
2337
\end{array}
$$

2337 is my answer." When told that half of 41 is 20½ and not 20, and that half of 5 is 2½ and not 2, Peter said he never bothers with fractions; they annoyed him so he gave them up.

Just to make sure that his teacher did not think him ready for a psychiatrist Peter multiplied 21 × 71 of his own accord thus:

$$
\begin{array}{r}
21 \times \ \ 71 \\
\cancel{10 \times \ \ 142} \\
5 \times \ \ 284 \\
\cancel{2 \times \ \ 568} \\
1 \times \underline{1136} \\
1491
\end{array}
$$

The only even numbers are 10 and 2, which he crossed out; adding up the rest, he got 1491, which you can verify by multiplying 21 by 71 in your way.

Peter is not as crazy as he seems. But what is behind it all and how does it work? It merely means that Peter was brought up in the *binary* system instead of the *decimal* system. Just as we have nine digits and a zero in our decimal system, Peter has only one digit and a zero in his binary system. In our system we write powers of 10 (10, 10 × 10, 10 × 10 × 10, etc.) as 1 followed by a number of zeros like this:

$$
\begin{array}{l}
10^1 = 10 \\
10^2 = 100 \\
10^3 = 1000 \\
10^4 = 10000 \text{ and so on}
\end{array}
$$

In Peter's system he does the same with powers of 2 (2, 2 × 2, 2 × 2 × 2, 2 × 2 × 2 × 2, etc.) which are written as 1 followed by a number of zeros thus:

$$2^1 = 1$$
$$2^2 = 10$$
$$2^3 = 100$$
$$2^4 = 1000$$
$$2^5 = 10000 \text{ and so on}$$

Our system is on the basis of 10. The tenth digit in our system is 1 plus a zero; Peter's system is on a basis of 2 so the second digit in his system is the same in appearance as the tenth digit in our system: namely, 10. Just as 11 is 10 + 1 in our system, so 3 is 11 in Peter's system because it is 2 (which he writes in the same way as our 10) plus 1. In Table 1 we have a complete translation up to our 64, from the binary system (which is Peter's system) to our own decimal system. Note we always add these powers of 2, putting down either 1 or zero. There is no digit higher than 1 in the binary system.

Note that in this table we have powers of 2 and of 10 across the top. Just as 10 is 10^1 so 2 is 2^1; just as 100 is 10^2 so 4 is 2^2; just as 1000 is 10^3 so 8 is 2^3; and so on. In the binary system, then, 2 is the same as 10 in the decimal system; 4 is the same as 100; 8 is the same as 1000; 16 is the same as 10000; and so on. To translate any decimal number into a binary number merely add these powers of 2 and refer to the decimal numbers under them: 53, for example, would be 32 + 16 + 4 + 1. Adding the numbers under these we get 100000 + 10000 + 100 + 1 or 110101, and this checks with the value for 53 given in the table. Note also that in the table each decimal number is divided into powers of 2 plus a remainder: 3 is not just 3 but $2^1 + 1$; 25 is not just 25 but $2^4 + 9$. This is because all powers of 2 in the binary system are written in the same way as powers of 10 in our decimal system.

Study this table carefully and see why 20 is 10100. Check this by adding 16 and 4 in the power table at the top. Now try 47,

TABLE 1

	1	2	4	8	16	32	64
	1	10	100	1000	10000	100000	1000000
3 = 2 + 1		11					
5 = 4 + 1			101				
6 = 4 + 2			110				
7 = 4 + 3			111				
9 = 8 + 1				1001			
10 = 8 + 2				1010			
11 = 8 + 3				1011			
12 = 8 + 4				1100			
13 = 8 + 5				1101			
14 = 8 + 6				1110			
15 = 8 + 7				1111			
17 = 16 + 1					10001		
18 = 16 + 2					10010		
19 = 16 + 3					10011		
20 = 16 + 4					10100		
21 = 16 + 5					10101		
22 = 16 + 6					10110		
23 = 16 + 7					10111		
24 = 16 + 8					11000		
25 = 16 + 9					11001		
26 = 16 + 10					11010		
27 = 16 + 11					11011		
28 = 16 + 12					11100		
29 = 16 + 13					11101		
30 = 16 + 14					11110		
31 = 16 + 15					11111		
33 = 32 + 1						100001	
34 = 32 + 2						100010	
35 = 32 + 3						100011	
36 = 32 + 4						100100	
37 = 32 + 5						100101	
38 = 32 + 6						100110	
39 = 32 + 7						100111	
40 = 32 + 8						101000	
41 = 32 + 9						101001	
42 = 32 + 10						101010	
43 = 32 + 11						101011	
44 = 32 + 12						101100	
45 = 32 + 13						101101	
46 = 32 + 14						101110	
47 = 32 + 15						101111	
48 = 32 + 16						110000	
49 = 32 + 17						110001	
50 = 32 + 18						110010	
51 = 32 + 19						110011	
52 = 32 + 20						110100	
53 = 32 + 21						110101	
54 = 32 + 22						110110	
55 = 32 + 23						110111	
56 = 32 + 24						111000	
57 = 32 + 25						111001	
58 = 32 + 26						111010	
59 = 32 + 27						111011	
60 = 32 + 28						111100	
61 = 32 + 29						111101	
62 = 32 + 30						111110	
63 = 32 + 31						111111	

36

which is 101111. Check this by adding 32, 8, 4, 2 and 1 in the same power table. Do the same with other binaries until you are thoroughly familiar with the system.

It is interesting to note that the number just before a new power is always composed of a number containing only the highest digits in the system. In the decimal system the highest digit is 9 and in the binary system it is 1. So we have by comparison:

DECIMAL	BINARY
99 is $(10^2 - 1)$	11 is $(2^2 - 1)$
999 is $(10^3 - 1)$	111 is $(2^3 - 1)$
9999 is $(10^4 - 1)$ and so on	1111 is $(2^4 - 1)$ and so on

Now, let us explain how Peter did his multiplication. To us it seems to be utter nonsense, but Peter says that our methods, with all the nine digits and things called fractions are much more complicated and ridiculous than his. He can't see why we use so many digits and why we complicate things with fractions. Whether we agree or not we must admit his binary system makes sense and always gives the correct result. Let's see how his multiplication system works. Let's take the previous example and examine it.

Remember Peter multiplied by 2 each time and so he gets the powers of 2 so important in the binary system. Remember also that Peter did away with all *even* numbers on the left column so if he just considers every other line, beginning with the first, he gets:

$$2^0 \times 71 = \quad 71$$
$$2^1 \times 71 = \quad 142 \text{ (eliminated)}$$
$$2^2 \times 71 = \quad 284$$
$$2^3 \times 71 = \quad 568 \text{ (eliminated)}$$
$$2^4 \times 71 = 1136$$

Now, in adding only the *odd* lines, which concern 2^0, 2^2 and 2^4, you will see by consulting the power table that his multiplier adds up to 21 $(1 + 4 + 16)$. By adding the results he has added $(2^0 \times 71) + (2^2 \times 71) + (2^4 \times 71)$ which, since $2^0 + 2^2 + 2^4 = 21$, is the same as saying 21×71. The sum of these, 1491, must be the same as the product of 21 and 71, and hence Peter is not as foolish as he seems.

Now you can see why Peter, in adding 14, 12 and 6 got 100000 and said it was 32, and why 4 × 6 in Peter's system comes out 11000, which is 24.

And you can also see how, since Babe Ruth in a single season once hit 60 home runs—that is, according to the decimal system—in Peter's binary system he hit 111100 of them; or, in other words, $2^2 + 2^3 + 2^4 + 2^5$. That makes $4 + 8 + 16 + 32 = 60$.

Let's take a few simple problems and work them out on the basis of 2 instead of 10. Let's multiply 7 × 3, for example. Consulting the table we see that 7 is $4 + 2 + 1$ which is 111. 3 is $2 + 1$ which is 11. Now multiply these binary numbers in the regular way.

$$
\begin{array}{r}
111 \ (4 + 2 + 1) \\
11 \ (2 + 1) \\
\hline
111 \\
111 \\
\hline
10101
\end{array}
$$

Note that in adding 1 and 1 we get 2, but 2 in our system is 10 in the binary system, so we put down the 0 and carry the 1. 1 and 1 again makes 2 and the 1 we carry makes 3, which in the binary system is 11. So we put down 1 and carry-over 1. The last 1 and 1 again is 10, which we put down and get 10101. Looking this up in the table we find that it is equal to 21 in our system, so, while 7 × 3 in our system is 21, in the binary system it's 10101.

Here is another, just for practice: 5 × 9. 5 is $4 + 1$ which is 101 from the table. 9 is $8 + 1$ which is 1001, hence:

$$
\begin{array}{r}
1001 \\
101 \\
\hline
1001 \\
1001 \\
\hline
101101
\end{array}
$$

101101 is 45 from the table.

Addition is just as simple. 15 + 16 + 2 equals 33 in our system. In the binary system it should equal 100001. Let's see if it does. 15 from the table is 1111, 16 is 10000, 2 is 10. Adding these we get:

$$
\begin{array}{rl}
15 = & 1111 \\
16 = & 10000 \\
2 = & \underline{10} \\
& 100001 = 33
\end{array}
$$

The binary system is vitally important because calculating machines of the more complicated type use it exclusively. These remarkable machines operate by means of punch holes in cards and flashing electronic tubes which are sensitive to changes so rapid we couldn't possibly see them or count them.

Since in the binary system we have *two and only two digits*, 1 and 0, you can see how the presence or absence of a punch hole in a card can determine either the 1 or the 0 (a hole would be 1 and no hole at all would be 0—or the other way round could be used). Any binary number can thus be punched on the card by a series of properly spaced holes. The decimal number 494, for example, which in binary language is 111101110, would be represented by punch holes in the card like this: 0 0 0 0 . 0 0 0 . The decimal number 50 would be 110010, which would be punched out like this: 0 0 . . 0 .

A similar arrangement holds for the electromagnetic relays, which are set up with negative (−) for 0 and positive (+) for 1. Thus every binary is a series of positive and negative pulsations which register in a flash. The number 2081, for example, is 100000100001 or + − − − − − + − − − − + ; this or any other number can be accurately flashed on and off in a fraction of a split second. The machine can multiply 29 by 36 in less time than you take to blink in the following way: 11101 × 100100 = 10000010100 and this result translates back into our decimal system as 1044. Here is a specimen of how, in a 50th of a second, 26 is multiplied by 19:

```
      11010
      10011
      11010
     11010
    1001110
    00000
    1001110
   00000
   01001110
  11010
  111101110  = 494
```

So amazingly rapid is the great Selective Sequence Electronic
Calculator of the International Business Machine Corporation
that it can multiply a number of 14 digits (in our decimal system)
by another such number of 14 digits in 1/50 of a second. Not
included, of course, is the time needed to set up the numbers in
the machine. It can also divide 33 pairs of 14-digit numbers in
one second and can add a 19-digit number to another 19-digit
number in 1/3500 of a second. It is all done on the binary system
and then translated back into our own decimal system. Obviously
if the machine had our ten digits to contend with it would never
be able to function with its speed and accuracy. The electromagnetic relay could not be just on or off; it would have to be
entirely off, 1/10 on, 2/10 on, 3/10 on and so forth, up to completely on. Something similar would have to be true for the holes
in the cards. The fact that the binary system has just two digits
eliminates this cumbersome system and enables the machine to
solve, in an hour, enormously difficult problems in higher mathematics that would take a mathematician or a scientist months to
do.

THE MAGIC OF NUMBERS

This Section on magic numbers and magic squares is by Royal V. Heath

ORDINARY NUMBERS have many fascinating and unusual properties. By arranging them in certain ways, thinking of them in different aspects, and even turning them upside down, we can make many puzzles and tricks, some of which are quite elaborate. In fact, a whole branch of the science of mathematics—number theory—might be thought of as the result of early number games and puzzles. In this section we'll present some lightning-calculator tricks, build some magic squares, and see what happens when numbers are turned upside down.

The Lightning Calculator

69	345	186	872	756
366	642	582	278	558
168	246	87	575	657
762	147	285	377	954
663	543	483	179	855
564	48	384	674	459

FIGURE 18

This is a trick which enables you to add up a column of figures faster than they can be written down. Have a friend select one number from each of the columns in this table and add them up. You will tell him the answer before he starts adding. This is

41

positively bewildering; no matter how many times you do it, or what numbers your friend selects, you will always give the correct answer.

Suppose, for example, your friend takes 366 from the first column, 147 from the second, 384 from the third, 872 from the fourth and 855 from the last column. All you have to do is to add the last digits of each (6, 7, 4, 2 and 5), and you get 24. Take this 24 from 50 and get 26. Now tack on the 24 and you get 2624, which is the answer.

It's extremely simple. Just add the last digits of each of the five numbers selected, take the result from 50, and that will be the first two digits in the answer. The last two digits will be the sum of the five last digits of the selected numbers which you already have and which you took from 50. That is all there is to it. Of course you must add mentally and quickly and nobody is supposed to know that you are even looking at these numbers— that is where the showmanship and mystery of the trick comes in.

What is the secret behind this trick? It lies in the way the numbers were chosen. Notice that in each column the middle digits are the same, and that the two end digits always add up to the same number. By picking these numbers properly, the trick is made to work every time.

Try another just to make sure you have it. Suppose the numbers selected are 168, 345, 483, 674 and 756. Your sum is 26. Take this from 50 and get 24. Tack on the 26 and the answer is 2426.

These Magic Numbers Add to 1952 in 14,400 Different Ways

Select any number at all from Figure 19. That number will be in some particular row and column. Now select any other number *not* in the same row or column as the previous number. Now select any remaining number *not* in the same row or column as either of the two previous numbers. Do the same for five different numbers so that each number you select will not be in the same row or column as any other number. You now have five numbers. If you add these five numbers you are sure to get 1952, the year this book was published.

Here is an example: Suppose you take 203 from column 1; that rules out all the numbers in column 1 and row 4. Now you take 280 from column 2. That rules out all the numbers from column 2 and row 2. Now take 391. That rules out all the numbers in

161	265	362	464	563
176	280	377	479	578
190	294	391	493	592
203	307	404	506	605
212	316	413	515	614

FIGURE 19

column 3 and row 3. You have very little choice left since you can't take any numbers that appear in rows 2, 3, or 4 or in columns 1, 2 and 3. Take 464 and the only remaining number available according to the rules is 614. You have now taken five numbers from five different rows and columns and they ought to add up to 1952. See if they do: 203 + 280 + 391 + 464 + 614 do add up to 1952. No matter which number you start with or which other numbers you choose, if you follow the rules you will always find the same answer: 1952.

It is very interesting to see how many ways we can get 1952 from this table. It can be figured out very easily, for:

We can take any one of the 25 numbers for the first number.

Eliminating one row and column, we can take any one of the 16 remaining numbers for the second number.

Removing another row and column, there are only 9 numbers left from which to choose the third number.

Only 4 numbers remain from which to choose the fourth number, and the last number is forced upon us by the rules.

Then, the total number of ways we can get 1952 from the table is:

$$5^2 + 4^2 + 3^2 + 2^2 + 1^2 \text{ or}$$
$$25 \times 16 \times 9 \times 4 \times 1 \text{ or } 14,400 \text{ different ways}$$

The Equality of Arithmetical Processes?

Here is what seems to be a proof that multiplication is the same as addition or subtraction and division is the same as addition or subtraction. If you can convince yourself that this is so it would naturally follow that multiplication is the same as division since they both equal the same things. Examine the following:

Multiplication	Addition
$1\frac{1}{2} \times 3$	$= 1\frac{1}{2} + 3 = 4\frac{1}{2}$
$1\frac{1}{3} \times 4$	$= 1\frac{1}{3} + 4 = 5\frac{1}{3}$
$1\frac{1}{4} \times 5$	$= 1\frac{1}{4} + 5 = 6\frac{1}{4}$
$1\frac{1}{5} \times 6$	$= 1\frac{1}{5} + 6 = 7\frac{1}{5}$
$1\frac{1}{6} \times 7$	$= 1\frac{1}{6} + 7 = 8\frac{1}{6}$

$$1\frac{1}{n} \times (n+1) = 1\frac{1}{n} + (n+1)$$

Multiplication	Subtraction
$1 \times \frac{1}{2}$	$= 1 - \frac{1}{2} = \frac{1}{2}$
$2 \times \frac{2}{3}$	$= 2 - \frac{2}{3} = 1\frac{1}{3}$
$3 \times \frac{3}{4}$	$= 3 - \frac{3}{4} = 2\frac{1}{4}$
$4 \times \frac{4}{5}$	$= 4 - \frac{4}{5} = 3\frac{1}{5}$
$5 \times \frac{5}{6}$	$= 5 - \frac{5}{6} = 4\frac{1}{6}$

$$n \times \frac{n}{n+1} = n - \frac{n}{n+1}$$

Division	Addition
$1\frac{1}{3} \div \frac{2}{3}$	$= 1\frac{1}{3} + \frac{2}{3} = 2$
$2\frac{1}{4} \div \frac{3}{4}$	$= 2\frac{1}{4} + \frac{3}{4} = 3$
$3\frac{1}{5} \div \frac{4}{5}$	$= 3\frac{1}{5} + \frac{4}{5} = 4$
$4\frac{1}{6} \div \frac{5}{6}$	$= 4\frac{1}{6} + \frac{5}{6} = 5$

$$\left(n + \frac{1}{n+2}\right) \div \frac{n+1}{n+2} = \left(n + \frac{1}{n+2}\right) + \frac{n+1}{n+2}$$

Division	Subtraction
$4\frac{1}{2} \div 3$	$= 4\frac{1}{2} - 3 = 1\frac{1}{2}$
$5\frac{1}{3} \div 4$	$= 5\frac{1}{3} - 4 = 1\frac{1}{3}$
$6\frac{1}{4} \div 5$	$= 6\frac{1}{4} - 5 = 1\frac{1}{4}$
$7\frac{1}{5} \div 6$	$= 7\frac{1}{5} - 6 = 1\frac{1}{5}$

$$\left(n + \frac{1}{n-2}\right) \div (n-1) = \left(n + \frac{1}{n-2}\right) - (n-1)$$

Some Equations Work Only Upside Down

It is mathematically impossible to find five numbers (all greater than zero) such that if we add them together and square the sum, the result will be equal to the sum of their squares. In other words, we cannot find five numbers A, B, C, D and E such that:

$$(A + B + C + D + E)^2 = A^2 + B^2 + C^2 + D^2 + E^2$$

You will see why this is true by multiplying out the left-hand side of the equation and canceling terms, because the equation demands that we find a series of positive numbers adding up to zero, which is impossible.

However, in the world of upside-down arithmetic many strange things are possible:

$$
\begin{array}{ccc}
1 & = & \overline{1} \\
1 & = & 1 \\
1 & = & 1 \\
3 & = & 9 \\
\underline{4} & = & 16
\end{array}
$$

FIGURE 20

In this example, the sum of the numbers in the first column is 10 and the square of 10 is 100. The numbers in the second column are the squares of those in the first column. If you turn this second column upside-down you will see that it adds up to 100. Hence the square of the sum of the numbers of the first column equals the sum of their squares (upside down) in the second column.

Upside-down Bigrade

When we play with numbers, very often we run across groups that have peculiar properties; not only are their sums equal (which can be arranged very easily), but also the sums of their *squares* are equal. Occasionally, even the sums of their *cubes* are equal! Such amazing groups of numbers are called *bigrades* or *trigrades*, depending upon whether their squares or cubes add up equally.

Figure 21 is a bigrade with an additional unusual property. The sum of the first three numbers equals the sum of the second three numbers. Both sums come to 253. But, since it is a bigrade,

$$69 + 98 + 86 = 96 + 68 + 89$$

FIGURE 21

the sum of the squares of the first three numbers also equals the sum of the squares of the second three numbers. Both sums add up to 21761. We then have:

$$68 + 89 + 96 = 98 + 86 + 69 = 253$$
$$68^2 + 89^2 + 96^2 = 98^2 + 86^2 + 69^2 = 21761$$

But that is not all. If you turn this bigrade upside down you will find that the same thing holds true. While the numbers have apparently changed, the sum of the first three still equals the sum of the second three, and the sums of their squares are also equal!

Some Equations Work in Different Directions

In Figure 22 we have a group of eight numbers that forms both a bigrade and a trigrade at the same time:

1. The sum of the first four equals the sum of the second four.
2. The sums of their squares are equal.
3. The sums of their cubes are equal.

However, in the case of this particular group, this is not only true when the numbers are held right side up but it is true also when they are held *upside down, in the mirror,* and *upside down in the mirror!*

The sums of each four numbers are equal to 19998.

The sums of their squares equal 149,494,950.

The sums of their cubes equal 1,242,200,007,576.

No matter how you look at it, the equation is correct!

Furthermore, if you study this bi- and trigrade you will see that you can group these numbers as follows:

$$\overset{A}{1181} + \overset{B}{1811} + \overset{B}{8188} + \overset{A}{8818} = \overset{C}{1118} + \overset{D}{1888} + \overset{D}{8111} + \overset{C}{8881}$$

FIGURE 22

46

If you do this you will see at once that:

Group $A + C =$ Group $B + D$
Group $B + C =$ Group $A + D$

The Melancholia Magic Square

The creator of this magic·square is unknown, but the square is shown in Dürer's famous 1514 engraving known as *Melancholia*. Figure 23 shows how Dürer depicted the square; if you examine the

FIGURE 23

magic square (made clearer in Figure 24) you will see some astounding things. In the first place, all rows, columns, and the two diagonals add up to the same number, just as in any ordinary similar magic square. Here the number is 34. In addition to this the four corner squares and the four center squares add up to 34. So do the opposite pairs of squares: 3 2 15 14, and 8 12 9 5, as well as the slanting squares 2 8 15 9, and 3 5 12 14. The corner sets of squares such as 9 6 15 4, 3 10 5 16, 2 13 8 11, and 12 1 14 7 all add up to 34.

But that is only the beginning. Note the date the painting was done, 1514, at the bottom of the square, and then observe the following:

The first eight numbers, written in numerical order are:

2 3 5 8 10 11 13 and 16

and their sum is equal to the second eight numbers

1 4 6 7 9 12 14 and 15

In other words the sum of all the numbers in the upper half (which is 68) is the same as the sum of all the numbers in the

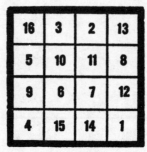

FIGURE 24

lower half. This is the case, of course, because each row sums to 34. But in addition to this the sums of the squares of these rows are equal or:

$$16 + 3 + 2 + 13 + 5 + 10 + 11 + 8 =$$
$$9 + 6 + 7 + 12 + 4 + 15 + 14 + 1 = 68$$

and

$$16^2 + 3^2 + 2^2 + 13^2 + 5^2 + 10^2 + 11^2 + 8^2 =$$
$$9^2 + 6^2 + 7^2 + 12^2 + 4^2 + 15^2 + 14^2 + 1^2 = 748$$

In addition, it is remarkable that the sum of the squares of alternate rows (the first and third, second and fourth) also add up to the same number. Here are the facts:

$$16 + 3 + 2 + 13 + 9 + 6 + 7 + 12 =$$
$$5 + 10 + 11 + 8 + 4 + 15 + 14 + 1 = 68$$

and

$$16^2 + 3^2 + 2^2 + 13^2 + 9^2 + 6^2 + 7^2 + 12^2 =$$
$$5^2 + 10^2 + 11^2 + 8^2 + 4^2 + 15^2 + 14^2 + 1^2 = 748$$

Also with respect to the columns, the sum of the first and second columns equals the sum of the third and fourth columns, and the sum of their squares is also equal, thus:

$$16 + 5 + 9 + 4 + 3 + 10 + 6 + 15 =$$
$$2 + 11 + 7 + 14 + 13 + 8 + 12 + 1 = 68$$

and

$$16^2 + 5^2 + 9^2 + 4^2 + 3^2 + 10^2 + 6^2 + 15^2 =$$
$$2^2 + 11^2 + 7^2 + 14^2 + 13^2 + 8^2 + 12^2 + 1^2 = 748$$

And the sum of the first and third columns equals the sum of the second and fourth columns and the sum of their squares is also equal, thus:

$$16 + 5 + 9 + 4 + 2 + 11 + 7 + 14 =$$
$$3 + 10 + 6 + 15 + 13 + 8 + 12 + 1 = 68$$

and

$$16^2 + 5^2 + 9^2 + 4^2 + 2^2 + 11^2 + 7^2 + 14^2 =$$
$$3^2 + 10^2 + 6^2 + 15^2 + 13^2 + 8^2 + 12^2 + 1^2 = 748$$

If the amazing facts stopped there this magic square would still be wonderful, but there is more. The numbers in the diagonals add up to the numbers not in the diagonals, and not only is the sum of their squares equal but the sum of their cubes is also equal! Thus:

$$16 + 10 + 7 + 1 + 4 + 6 + 11 + 13 =$$
$$2 + 8 + 12 + 14 + 15 + 9 + 5 + 3 = 68$$

and

$$16^2 + 10^2 + 7^2 + 1^2 + 4^2 + 6^2 + 11^2 + 13^2 =$$
$$2^2 + 8^2 + 12^2 + 14^2 + 15^2 + 9^2 + 5^2 + 3^2 = 748$$

and

$$16^3 + 10^3 + 7^3 + 1^3 + 4^3 + 6^3 + 11^3 + 13^3 =$$
$$2^3 + 8^3 + 12^3 + 14^3 + 15^3 + 9^3 + 5^3 + 3^3 = 9248$$

It is also interesting to note that, symmetrically:

$$2 + 8 + 9 + 15 = 3 + 5 + 12 + 14 = 34$$
$$2^2 + 8^2 + 9^2 + 15^2 = 3^2 + 5^2 + 12^2 + 14^2 = 374$$
$$2^3 + 8^3 + 9^3 + 15^3 = 3^3 + 5^3 + 12^3 + 14^3 = 4624$$

This is truly a marvelous magic square. Every row, column and the two diagonals add up to 34. The four corner squares, the four center squares, the four opposite squares both vertically and horizontally, the four symmetrical squares (2 8 9 15) as well as the other four (3 5 12 14) also add up to 34. Not only that, but each corner group of four squares like 16 3 10 5 adds up to 34. In addition to all of this we see that the sum of the first two rows equals the sum of the bottom two rows and the sum of the squares of the numbers in the first two rows equals the sum of the squares of the numbers of the bottom two rows. The same is true for sum of the numbers of the first and third rows (and the sum of their squares) as respects the numbers of the second and fourth rows. What has been said of the rows applies also to the columns. The sum of the numbers and the sum of their squares in the first two columns equals the sum of the numbers and the sum of their squares in the last two columns. The numbers of the first and third columns, summed or squared, equal in the same way the numbers of the second and fourth columns, summed or squared. In addition to all this, the numbers in the diagonals, as well as their squares and cubes, add up to the same amounts as the numbers not in the diagonals and their squares and cubes. This amazing fact also holds true for the four numbers symmetrically placed as given above. Finally, if you add each upper and lower pair of numbers vertically or horizontally, you will have patterns as follows:

Horizontal:	21	13	13	21	*Vertical:*	19	15
	13	21	21	13		15	19
						15	19
						19	15

While this magic square of Dürer, painted in the sixteenth century, has been seen by millions of people it has never before been analyzed so closely with regard to multigrades.

The construction of this magic square is quite simple. If you take a square of sixteen cells and lightly draw the diagonals you will have the general principle. Start at the top square with 16 and *count backwards*, placing the numbers only in the squares which the diagonals pass through. You will then have:

16	.	.	13
.	11	10	.
.	7	6	.
4	.	.	1

Now go back to the top row and fill in the missing numbers wherever there is an empty space, *counting forwards* from small numbers to large. The first space is filled so you skip it and put 2 and 3 in the next two. Continuing in this way with 5 and 8 in the second row, and so on, you will have the finished square:

16	2	3	13
5	11	10	8
9	7	6	12
4	14	15	1

This is essentially the same as the Dürer square but, in order to satisfy the date of painting the numbers 14 and 15 were interchanged, and consequently the two columns in which they stand also had to be interchanged. Of course this does not affect any of the relationships we have discussed, because of the way in which the numbers in the two inside columns compensate for each other.

Upside-down Magic Square

Figure 25 shows a remarkable magic square. The two diagonals and every row and column add up to 264. Now look at Figure 26, in which letters are used to indicate the squares in the magic square diagram. You will see that squares *A*, *B*, *C* and *D*, the four corner squares, add up to 264. So do squares *E*, *F*, *G* and *H*; *I*, *J*, *L* and *K*; *E*, *I*, *H* and *L*; *J*, *G*, *K* and *F*; *M*, *N*, *P* and *O*, as well as most of the small squares such as *A*, *I*, *M* and *E*; *J*, *B*, *N* and *G*; *E*, *M*, *O* and *F*; *N*, *G*, *H* and *P*, and many many more. They each add up to 264.

Now if you turn this magic square upside-down you will see that, in spite of the fact that the numbers are different and are in different positions, they nevertheless still add up to the same 264 in the same way. There are about 48 ways of making 264 from this 4-cell magic square.

96	11	89	68
88	69	91	16
61	86	18	99
19	98	66	81

FIGURE 25

A	I	J	B
E	M	N	G
F	O	P	H
C	K	L	D

FIGURE 26

IXOHOXI

An Amazing Magic Square

This is a most unusual name and it represents a most unusual magic square. It is pronounced *Ixo-hocksie* and you will see at once that the name is the same backwards as forwards, upside down as right side up, in the mirror upside down as well as right side up. No matter how you hold it or look at it, it will always be IXOHOXI (Figure 27).

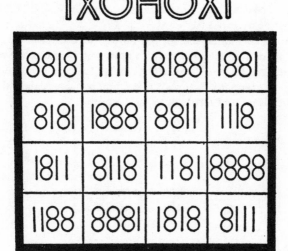

FIGURE 27

Now the same is true for the magic square it represents. Like all other magic squares all rows, columns and the two diagonals add up to the same number—in this case it is 19998. But that is not all. If you refer to Figure 28, in which letters are used to indicate the position of the squares in IXOHOXI, you will see that the four corner squares *A, B, D* and *C* each add up to 19998.

So do squares *E, F, G* and *H; I, J, L* and *K; J, B, D* and *L; E, I, H* and *L; J, G, K* and *F*. In addition to all this, each small square inside IXOHOXI, such as *A, I, M* and *E; I, J, N* and *M; J, B, G* and *N; E, M, O* and *F*, and each of the others, adds up to 19998.

Now if you turn IXOHOXI upside down the same thing holds true. All the rows, columns, diagonals and the same squares as previously mentioned each add up to 19998. There are more than 25 ways of making 19998 in each position so we have more than 50 ways when holding IXOHOXI right side up and upside down.

And the exact thing is true all over again if you hold IXOHOXI up to the mirror. You will see that 19998 is the total of each of the rows, columns, diagonals and the squares previously discussed. And if you turn the square upside down and read it in the mirror the result is the same! IXOHOXI makes 19998 in more than 100 ways. It makes this sum right side up, upside down, right side up in the mirror and upside down in the mirror.

FIGURE 28

Crossword Magic Square

This is a combination of a peculiar form of crossword puzzle with a distorted magic square. If you follow the directions, filling in Figure 29 according to the definitions given, and following through, the result will be a number-"crossword" in which every row, column, diagonal and small square adds up to 42. Do the puzzle and then check your answer with that in the back of the book. Here are the definitions:

1. *It makes packages secure* (6 letters). Place the letters in these squares respectively: 14, 9, 15, 11, 2 and 5.

2. *Something used in a classroom.* It's white and has 5 letters. Place these letters in the following squares: 18, 3, 13, 7 and 12.

FIGURE 29

3. *An unruly crowd* (3 letters). Place these letters in squares 6, 1 and 10 respectively.

4. *Past tense of feed* (3 letters). Place these letters in boxes 17, 4 and 16.

5. Abbreviation for *Justice of the Peace* (2 letters). Place these letters in squares 8 and 20.

6. The last is the only letter of the alphabet that is always followed by U, and is placed in square 19.

If you have completed the crossword puzzle properly the diagram will not contain any words at all, and each square will contain a different letter.

After you have done this, place the number of each letter as it appears in the alphabet (*A*—1, *B*—2, *C*—3, etc.) in the corresponding square in Figure 30. For example, square number 13

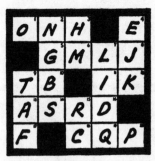

FIGURE 30

should contain the letter *A*, and thus you would write the number 1 in the corresponding square.

After you have finished transferring all of the letters of Figure 29 to numbers in Figure 30 you will have a magic square all of whose rows, columns, diagonals and small squares add up to 42. The correct magic square appears on page 175.

OTHER NUMBER FACTS AND CURIOSITIES

CASTING OUT NINES

THIS INTERESTING and well-known method is used for checking addition and multiplication quickly. We add the digits repeatedly to each other until we arrive at a single digit, the digit 9 being regarded as equal to zero. For example:

$$3471 = 3 + 4 + 7 + 1 = 15 = 5 + 1 = 6$$
$$477 = 4 + 7 + 7 = 18 = 8 + 1 = 9 = 0$$

Now let us apply this system to addition and multiplication. If the addition of the digits in the answer agrees with the addition of the digits separately, the sum is correct.

$$
\begin{array}{rcl}
437 &=& 14 = 5 \\
8162 &=& 17 = 8 \\
9217 &=& 19 = 1 \\
378 &=& 18 = 0 \\
\hline
18194 & & 14 = 5 \\
\end{array}
$$

$$1 + 8 + 1 + 9 + 4 = 23 = 5$$ } Final digits the same

$$
\begin{array}{rcl}
517 &=& 13 = 4 \\
368 &=& 17 = 8 \\
923 &=& 14 = 5 \\
416 &=& 11 = 2 \\
\hline
2224 & & 19 = 10 = 1 \\
\end{array}
$$

$$2 + 2 + 2 + 4 = 10 = 1$$ } Final digits the same

In multiplication:

$$
\begin{array}{rcl}
14963 &=& 23 = 5 \\
\underline{371} &=& 11 = \underline{2} \\
14963 && \overline{10} = 1 \\
104741 \\
\underline{44889} \\
5551273 &=& 28 = 10 = 1
\end{array}
$$

Final digits the same

$$
\begin{array}{rcl}
59761 &=& 28 = 10 = 1 \\
\underline{417} &=& 12 = 3; 3 \times 1 = 3 \\
418327 \\
59761 \\
\underline{239044} \\
24920337 &=& 30 = 3
\end{array}
$$

Final digits the same

Applying this to subtraction, we get:

$$
\begin{array}{rcl}
1473165 &=& 27 = 9 \\
\underline{588232} &=& 28 = \underline{1} \\
884933 && 8
\end{array}
$$

$$8 + 8 + 4 + 9 + 3 + 3 = 35 = 8$$

Final digits the same

OBVIOUS BUT INTERESTING

CONSIDER A number like 435 or 46853 in which the center digit is not 9 and the sum of the remaining digits is 9 or a multiple of 9. Add all the digits and if the sum is written with more than one digit add the digits of the sum until only one digit remains. That remaining digit will always be the middle digit. For example:

Add the digits in 435 and you get 12. Add these two and get 3 which is the middle number in 435. Add the digits in 46853 and the result is 26. Add 2 and 6 and get 8, the middle digit. 631857254 has digits adding up to 41. Add 4 and 1 and get 5, the middle digit.

The reason for this is obvious but interesting. Each number must have an odd number of digits with a digit (not 9) in the center.

Since the sum of all the digits repeatedly added is a multiple of 9 we have the simple formula:

$n(10 - 1) + k$, where k is the middle digit and 9 is $10 - 1$.

This is $10n - n + k$, and if you add the 1 and 0 of the 10 you get $1n$ or n. Now $n - n + k = k$, the middle digit.

INTERESTING IDENTITIES

Note the following:

$$3^4 + 4^4 + 5^4 = 5^2 + 19^2 + 24^2$$
$$3^8 + 4^8 + 5^8 = 5^4 + 19^4 + 24^4$$

$$7^2 + 34^2 + 41^2 = 14^2 + 29^2 + 43^2$$
$$7^4 + 34^4 + 41^4 = 14^4 + 29^4 + 43^4$$

These identities are most unusual. It is very difficult to find three numbers a b and c such that $a^n + b^n + c^n$ and $a^{2n} + b^{2n} + c^{2n}$ equal $d^{\frac{n}{2}} + e^{\frac{n}{2}} + f^{\frac{n}{2}}$ and $d^n + e^n + f^n$ respectively.

MAGIC NUMBERS

THE RECIPROCALS of certain prime numbers have very interesting properties and lend themselves to baffling mathematical tricks, like multiplying 16 or 28 digits by one or two digits in your head as fast as anyone can write them down.

Of the reciprocals of prime numbers from 1 to 1/31, three— 1/7, 1/17 and 1/29—show these remarkable properties. Let us consider 1/7 first. In decimal form it is .142857142857 ... Note that it repeats itself after six digits and keeps on indefinitely in the same sequence 142857. Now no matter what number you multiply this 142857 by from 1 to and including 6, you will always get the same sequence of digits in the answer thus:

$$1 \times 142857 = 142857$$
$$2 \times 142857 = 285714$$
$$3 \times 142857 = 428571$$
$$4 \times 142857 = 571428$$
$$5 \times 142857 = 714285$$
$$6 \times 142857 = 857142$$

and, of course 7 × 142857 is 999999. Note that all the digits in the above answers are the same and in the same sequence as 142857. In the first case of 2 × 142857 we start with 28 because 2 × 14 is 28. Starting with 28 we run the number through until we come back to 28, and so we get 285714. In the case of 3 × 142857, we know that 3 × 14 is 42; hence we start with the 42 and run the number through, getting 428571. And so it is for the other digits as you can see: 4 × 142857 starts at 57 since 4 × 14 is 56 (which is nearer to 57 than to any other pair in the sequence), and we get 571428. The digits never vary in their sequence. It is interesting to note that the sum of these answers is 2857140 which still contains the same digits in the same sequence.

The next reciprocal of a prime number that we consider is 1/17, which is more complicated but much more interesting. It turns out to be .05882352941176470. Omitting the first zero, we see that it has sixteen places without repeating itself just as 1/7 had six places without repeating itself. Now you can multiply this large number by any number from 1 to 16 inclusive and the answer will always have the same digits in the same order just as in the case of 1/7. Of course 5882352941176470 × 17 = 99999-9999999999990. Now consider:

$$2 \times 5882352941176470 = 11764705882352940$$
$$3 \times 5882352941176470 = 17647058823529410$$
$$4 \times 5882352941176470 = 23529411764705880$$
$$5 \times 5882352941176470 = 29411764705882350$$
$$6 \times 5882352941176470 = 35294117647058820$$
$$9 \times 5882352941176470 = 52941176470588230$$
$$11 \times 5882352941176470 = 64705882352941170$$

A little study of these answers will show you that the same digits always appear and in the same sequence, but of course the starting number is different in each case. Since 58, call it 5.8, which begins the 5882352941176470, is a "little less than 6," any number we multiply this big number by, from 1 to and including 16, must start at a little less than 6 times that number. In other words: 2 × 6 is 12. Start at 11 ("a little less than 12") in that big number and run the digits through until you come back to 11. In the same way 3 × 6 is a little less than 18, so find 17 in the big number and that is your starting point. Note that this holds true right along: 4 × 5882352941176470 starts at 23 since 4 × 6 is 24 and we start "a little less" than 4 × 6; 5 × 5882352941176470 starts at 29; 6 × 5882352941176470 starts at 35, and so on. Note that a zero is always added to the very last digit.

It is very easy to memorize this large number merely by taking it in groups of 3 thus: 588, 235, 294, 117, 6470. Just repeat these groups ten or fifteen times to yourself and you will have them memorized with but little effort. You will be able to rattle off this large number starting at any particular place and can therefore multiply it by any digit from 1 to 16 inclusive entirely in your head, much to the amazement of your friends.

Suppose you write this number on a sheet of paper and, without looking at it again, ask a friend to multiply it by any digit between 1 and 17. You can tell him the answer in a flash. Suppose he says "Multiply it by 7." You say to yourself "7 × 6 is 42, so start at 41 and run the number through." You say out loud "41176470588235290," which is the correct answer.

After you have mastered that number you can, if you want, go on to bigger numbers such as the reciprocal of 29, which is:

$$3448275862068965517241379310$$

which, of course, has 28 places before it starts to repeat. This giant can be multiplied by any number from 1 to and including 28 and you will have the same kind of result as you did with the previous number—the digits will always be the same in the answer and in the same sequence, thus:

34482758620689655172413793310 × 2 = 6896551724137931034482758620
34482758620689655172413793310 × 5 = 17241379310344827586206896550

Notice that here the starting numbers on the giant are 344, which is a little less than $3\frac{1}{2}$; hence we multiply our multiplier by $3\frac{1}{2}$ and look for a pair of digits a little less than that result. 2 × 344 is a little less than 2 × $3\frac{1}{2}$, so start at 68. 5 × $3\frac{1}{2}$ is $17\frac{1}{2}$, so start at 17 in the large number. The entire principle is the same as with the previous numbers but much more impressive.

MULTIPLYING WITHOUT REPEATING DIGITS

LONG WORDS without repetition of letters are rare. A few of these are: PLAYGROUNDS, DUMBWAITERS, WORKMANSHIP, REPUBLICANS, and SYMPATHIZER. More difficult to find are 8-digit numbers without repetition of digits which, when multiplied by the number 9, give nine-digit numbers also without repetition of digits. Here are four such numbers:

58132764   72645831   76125483   81274365

Notice that no digit is repeated in any of these numbers and 9 is missing in all of them. If each of these numbers is now multiplied by 9 the result is respectively:

523194876   653812479   685129347   731469285

Still more unusual is the fact that if each of these numbers is multiplied by 18 the result is a 10-digit number, with no digit repeated, thus:

58132764 × 18 = 1046389752
72645831 × 18 = 1307624958
76125483 × 18 = 1370258694
81274365 × 18 = 1462938570

REVERSED-DIGIT PLAYGROUND

ADDITION SEEMS to be the reverse of multiplication in. the following:

$$9 + 9 = 18 = 9 \times 9 = 81$$
$$24 + 3 = 27 = 24 \times 3 = 72$$
$$47 + 2 = 49 = 47 \times 2 = 94$$
$$497 + 2 = 499 = 497 \times 2 = 994$$

RARE PRIME DECADES

A DECADE IN this case is a set of ten continuous numbers. The first decade is from 1 to 10 inclusive, the second decade from 11 to 20 and so on. In each such decade there can never be more than four prime numbers. In the vast percentage of cases the number of primes in a decade is two or three and four primes are quite rare. For example from 31 to 40 we have 31 and 37 as the only primes. From 41 to 50 we have 41, 43 and 47. Very seldom indeed do four primes appear in a decade, but here is a list of such cases up to 5,000:

2	3	5	7	1481	1483	1487	1489
11	13	17	19	1871	1873	1877	1879
101	103	107	109	2081	2083	2087	2089
191	193	197	199	3251	3253	3257	3259
821	823	827	829	3461	3463	3467	3469

The rarity of four primes in a decade is due to the fact that there are only four possible numbers in a decade that can be prime. In each decade there are 5 even numbers which, with the exception of 2, can never be prime, and five odd numbers. Of the five odd numbers there is always a multiple of 5 such as 45, 65, 75, etc., and, of course, this cannot be prime. The remaining four numbers must end in 1, 3, 7 and 9, no matter how large they are, and often one or another of these is divisible by 3 or 7 or 9, such as, for example, 63, 49, 57, etc.

MAGIC MULTIPLICATION SQUARE

HERE IS an extremely unique magic square devised by Alfred Moessner. Instead of adding the rows and columns we multiply them and the same answer results each time. Every row and column gives 120 for the answer when the numbers are multiplied.

1	12	10
15	2	4
8	5	3

FIBONACCI NUMBERS

THIS REMARKABLE series, published in 1202 by Leonardo of Pisa (also known as Fibonacci), has an almost endless variety of fascinating features. As you can see, each term in the series is the sum of the two preceding terms. If you take the sum or the difference of consecutive terms you will get the same series over and over again. Here is the series:

1 1 2 3 5 8 13 21 34 55 89 144 233 377 610 987 1597 . . .

1. Now take any term in the series and call it A_n and we have the following:

$$A_n \times A_{n+1} = A_{n-1} \times A_{n+2} \pm 1 \quad \text{(Any term} \times \text{the following term} =$$
$$A_n \times A_{n+1} = A_{n-2} \times A_{n+3} \pm 2 \quad \text{the preceding term} \times \text{the second}$$
$$A_n \times A_{n+1}{}^1 = A_{n-3} \times A_{n+4} \pm 6 \quad \text{term following} \pm 1)$$
$$A_n \times A_{n+1} = A_{n-4} \times A_{n+5} \pm 15 \quad \text{etc.}$$

Let's test this. Take any term for A_n, as for example 13. Then 13 × 21 should be equal to 8 × 34 ± 1: 13 × 21 = 273; 8 × 34 = 272. The relationship applies throughout the series; you can test it with any other pair like 34 × 55 = 21 × 89 ± 1. If A_n is an even term in the series, the 1 is subtracted; if A_n is an odd term the 1 is added. In the first example, 13 is the seventh term (odd), and therefore the 8 × 34 had 1 added. In the case of 3 × 5 equals 2 × 8 − 1, 3 is the fourth term (even) and hence the 1 is subtracted. In the second example given (34 × 55) we know that 34 is the ninth term in the series (odd); therefore the result will be 21 × 89 + 1.

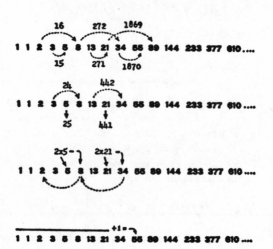

1 1 2 3 5 8 13 21 34 55 89 144 233 377 610

Reasoning the same way we can take the second set above, namely:

$$A_n \times A_{n+1} = A_{n-2} \times A_{n+3} \pm 2$$

Let's take 8 as A_n; then 8×13 should equal $3 \times 34 \pm 2$ and it does; since 8 is the sixth term in the series (even), the 2 is subtracted. Take 89×144. This should equal $34 \times 377 \pm 2$ and since 89 is the eleventh term (odd), the 2 must be added: $89 \times 144 = 12816$ and $34 \times 377 = 12818$.

There is no need to go further. The other sets of equations work out in exactly the same way. You will notice that we have some very interesting plus and minus figures in the above formulas—in order, they are:

$$\pm 1 \quad \pm 2 \quad \pm 6 \quad \pm 15 \quad \pm 40 \quad \pm 104 \quad \ldots$$

The difference between these numbers is;

$$1 \quad 4 \quad 9 \quad 25 \quad 64 \quad \ldots$$
$$1^2 \quad 2^2 \quad 3^2 \quad 5^2 \quad 8^2 \quad \ldots$$

This is nothing more than the square of the Fibonacci terms!

2. Now we'll try something else. Let us examine the following and then make tests as we did with the previous equations:

$$A_{n-1} \times A_{n+1} = A_n^2 \pm 1 = 1^2$$
$$A_{n-2} \times A_{n+2} = A_n^2 \pm 1 = 1^2$$
$$A_{n-3} \times A_{n+3} = A_n^2 \pm 4 = 2^2$$
$$A_{n-4} \times A_{n+4} = A_n^2 \pm 9 = 3^2$$
$$A_{n-5} \times A_{n+5} = A_n^2 \pm 25 = 5^2$$
$$A_{n-6} \times A_{n+6} = A_n^2 \pm 64 = 8^2$$
$$\ldots\ldots\ldots\ldots\ldots\ldots\ldots\ldots$$

In the square of any term, $A_n^2 \pm 1$ is equal to the product of the term before it and the term after it: $5^2 - 1$ equals 3×8; $21^2 + 1$ equals 13×34, as you can verify from the following repetition of the Fibonacci series:

1 1 2 3 5 8 13 21 34 55 89 144 233 377 610 987 1597 . . .

You can test all the other equations in the same way, always by letting A_n be any term, A_{n+1} be the term following, and A_{n-1} the term preceding. You will note again that the plus and minus numbers 1 1 4 9 25 64 . . . are the squares of the Fibonacci numbers.

3. Now let us write the squares of each term of the Fibonacci series. We then have:

1 4 9 25 64 169 441 1156 3025 7921 . . .

Adding each pair we get: 5 13 34 89 233 610 1597 . . . or the odd terms in the Fibonacci series. Subtracting each of these terms from the following term, we get the even terms, thus: 8 21 55 144 377 . . .

4. Now let us consider the series again from a different standpoint:

1 1 2 3 5 8 13 21 34 55 89 144 233 377 610 987 1597 . . .

You will find that twice any term minus the following term is the second term preceding:

$$2 \times A_n - A_n + 1 = A_n - 2$$

Take 5. Twice 5 is 10 minus 8 equals 2. Take 55: 110 − 89 = 21.

5. If we add up the terms in the Fibonacci series as we go along we get 1 2 4 7 12 20 33 54 88 143 232 376 . . . Each term in this series is 1 less than the term located two steps further on in the Fibonacci series. A startling trick in "lightning addition" can be made from this fact. Put down all the Fibonacci numbers in a column. Now go down the column and draw a line anywhere. The sum of all the numbers above that line will equal one less than the second number below it. In the column shown here, suppose you draw a line under 13. The sum of all the numbers above that line will be 33, or one less than 34. The numbers above 610 will be 1596, which you can tell instantly if you carry the series out that far in a single column, thus:

This trick will certainly mystify your friends who are not familiar with the Fibonacci series. The numbers here look as though they were picked at random.

6. Let us identify any four consecutive terms in the Fibonacci series by the letters *a, b, c, d.* Now let *n* be the numerical place of *a* in the series, so that, if *a* = 3 (the *fourth* number of the series), *n* = 4. Then it happens that:

$$(2bc)^2 + (ad)^2 = (A_{2n+3})^2$$

where *A* is the number standing at the numerical place in the

1
1
2
3
5
8
13
21
34
55
89
144
233
377
610
987
1597
2584

series indicated by $2n + 3$. This is an amazing equation discovered by Dr. J. Ginsburg. Let us examine it closely. We repeat the series:

1 1 2 3 5 8 13 21 34 55 89 144 233 377 610 987 . . .

Take the four terms 3, 5, 8 and 13. Then, by the formula:
$(2 \times 5 \times 8)^2 + (3 \times 13)^2 = 89^2$. Why 89? Because n in this case is 4 (3 is the fourth term of the series) and $2n + 3$ is therefore 11. The eleventh term of the series is 89.

In the same way 2, 3, 5 and 8 give:
$(2 \times 3 \times 5)^2 + (2 \times 8)^2 = 34$. Why 34? Because n—the position of 2 in the series—in this case is 3, so that $2n + 3 = 9$. The ninth term of the series is 34. It is interesting that if $2bc$ and ad are considered to be the sides of a right triangle, then $2n + 3$ will be its hypotenuse.

7. The eleventh term of the Fibonacci series is remarkable in itself, as Professor Jekuthiel Ginsburg points out. Its reciprocal (1/89) happens to be a Fibonacci number series all by itself. This is quite amazing; here it is worked out for you:

$$\frac{1}{89} = \begin{cases} .0112358 \\ \quad\quad 13 \\ \quad\quad\quad 21 \\ \quad\quad\quad\quad 34 \\ \quad\quad\quad\quad\quad 55 \\ \quad\quad\quad\quad\quad\quad 89 \\ \quad\quad\quad\quad\quad\quad\, 144 \\ \quad\quad\quad\quad\quad\quad\quad 233 \ldots \\ \overline{.011235955040673 \ldots} \end{cases}$$

8. Dr. Jekuthiel Ginsburg shows that in three successive Fibonacci numbers A_n, A_{n+1} and A_{n+2} the sum of the cubes of the two greater ones minus the cube of the smallest one is always a Fibonacci number. You can easily test this from the Fibonacci series:

1 1 2 3 5 8 13 21 34 55 89 144 233 377 610 987 . . .

Take 8, 5 and 3, for example: $8^3 + 5^3 - 3^3 = 512 + 125 - 27 = 610$.

Or take 13, 8 and 5: $13^3 + 8^3 - 5^3 = 2197 + 512 - 125 = 2584$. Both 610 and 2584 belong in the series.

9. The famous Golden Section, which the Greeks used so extensively in their art and architecture, is the irrational number 1.61805 . . . which is expressed as the value of x in the quadratic equation $x^2 = 1 + x$, and turns out to be $\frac{1}{2}(1 + \sqrt{5})$. It is amazing to find this famous ratio popping up in the Fibonacci series. As you multiply each term in the series by 1.618 . . . it comes nearer and nearer to the exact value of the next term:

$$1 \times 1.618 \ldots = \quad 1.618 \text{ which is } \quad 2 - .392$$
$$2 \times 1.618 \ldots = \quad 3.236 \text{ which is } \quad 3 + .236$$
$$3 \times 1.618 \ldots = \quad 4.854 \text{ which is } \quad 5 - .146$$
$$5 \times 1.618 \ldots = \quad 8.090 \text{ which is } \quad 8 + .090$$
$$8 \times 1.618 \ldots = \quad 12.944 \text{ which is } 13 - .056$$
$$13 \times 1.618 \ldots = \quad 21.034 \text{ which is } 21 + .034$$
$$21 \times 1.618 \ldots = \quad 33.978 \text{ which is } 34 - .022$$
$$34 \times 1.618 \ldots = \quad 55.012 \text{ which is } 55 + .012$$
$$\cdot \quad \cdot \quad \cdot \quad \cdot \quad \cdot \quad \cdot \quad \cdot \quad \cdot \quad \cdot \quad \cdot \quad \cdot \quad \cdot \quad \cdot$$
$$144 \times 1.618 \ldots = 232.992 \text{ which is } 233 - .008$$

POWERS

POWERS

THE LAST digits of the powers of numbers shows a regular pattern. For one thing they keep repeating, never varying, and the second and fourth powers show a regular symmetry while the last digit of the fifth power is the same as that of the number itself. Consider the table on page 72. The numbers are shown in the first column, extending up to 20. The second column shows the last digit of the squares of these numbers, the third column the last digit of the cubes, the fourth column the last digit of the fourth powers and so on up to the ninth power. Note, in the square column, the symmetry of 1 4 9 6 5 6 9 4 1 0 and its repetition, which keeps on forever. In the cube column all the nine digits are represented, although there is no definite symmetry. In the fourth-power column we have the 1 6 1 6 5 6 1 6 1 0 symmetry and in the fifth-power column we have the regular sequence of the numbers, the same as the first ten in the number column. With the fifth-power column, the kinds of series are complete: all these powers keep on repeating forever, as you can readily verify. The sixth column is the same as the square column and the seventh column the same as the cube, and so on.

And the larger numbers repeat the smaller ones. The square of 62 ends in 4, just as does that of any other number whose digits end in 2. The cube of 62 has to end in 8 and its fourth power in 6, and so on. Ruling out the sixth and tenth rows, whose powers always end in 6 (or in 0), you will find that the sum of the first four digits in the other first ten rows each adds up to 20. This, of course, is repeated in the second group of ten rows, and so on forever. Now compare rows 2 and 8 and rows 3 and 7 and you'll see the same digits in different arrangements.

NO.	SQ.	CUBE	FOURTH	FIFTH	SIXTH	SEVENTH	EIGHTH	NINTH
1	1	1	1	1	1	1	1	1
2	4	8	6	2	4	8	6	2
3	9	7	1	3	9	7	1	3
4	6	4	6	4	6	4	6	4
5	5	5	5	5	5	5	5	5
6	6	6	6	6	6	6	6	6
7	9	3	1	7	9	3	1	7
8	4	2	6	8	4	2	6	8
9	1	9	1	9	1	9	1	9
10	0	0	0	0	0	0	0	0
11	1	1	1	1	1	1	1	1
12	4	8	6	2	4	8	6	2
13	9	7	1	3	9	7	1	3
14	6	4	6	4	6	4	6	4
15	5	5	5	5	5	5	5	5
16	6	6	6	6	6	6	6	6
17	9	3	1	7	9	3	1	7
18	4	2	6	8	4	2	6	8
19	1	9	1	9	1	9	1	9
20	0	0	0	0	0	0	0	0

THE SUM OF THE CONSECUTIVE ODD NUMBERS IS A SQUARE

IT IS AN interesting fact, easily proved, that the sum of the first n terms of odd numbers is always a perfect square. You can see this clearly from this progression of odd numbers:

$$1 \quad 3 \quad 5 \quad 7 \quad 9 \quad 11 \quad 13 \quad 15 \quad 17 \quad 19 \quad 21 \quad . \quad . \quad .$$

The sum of the first 2 is 4 or 2^2
The sum of the first 3 is 9 or 3^2
The sum of the first 4 is 16 or 4^2

The sum of the first 5 is 25 or 5^2

. . . .

The sum of the first n is n^2

The reason for this is quite simple. In the arithmetic progression formula for the sum we have:

$$S = \frac{n}{2}[2a + (n-1)d]$$

where a is 1 and d is 2, since a is the first term and d is the difference in the terms. This develops into $S = \frac{n}{2}(2 + 2n - 2)$ which equals $\frac{2n^2}{2}$ or n^2.

SQUARE ROOTS BY THE PYTHAGOREAN THEOREM

FIGURE 31 shows an interesting way to obtain the square roots of numbers by the right-triangle method. If an isosceles right triangle is drawn with unity for the equal sides, as shown, the hypotenuse will be the square root of 2. Note that the horizontal side of the triangle is divided into tenths and that the radius of 1 projected on the hypotenuse leaves a balance of .41 . . . The square root of 2 is actually 1.41 . . . Now, with the square root of 2 as a base and the other side equal to unity, construct another right triangle. The hypotenuse of this new triangle will have to be the square root of 3 since it is the square root of $2 + 1^2$. Now the square root of 3 is actually 1.73 . . . and this may be roughly verified by referring to the portion left over after the radius of 1 is taken out. The next triangle has the square root of 3 for its base and 1 for its side and its hypotenuse is therefore the square root of 4 which is 2 units.

Continuing in this way we can get the square roots of 5, 6, 7, 8, 9, 10 and any other number quickly and easily. Note the second radius of 2 (the square root of 4) cutting all the triangles

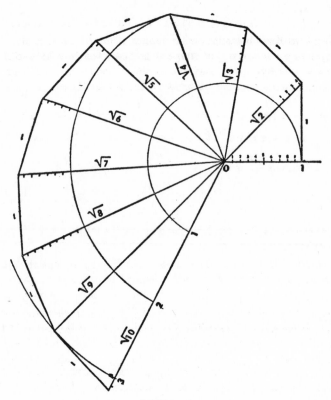

FIGURE 31

after the third, and the radius of 3 appearing after the triangle with a base of the square root of 9. You can continue this indefinitely and you will find that the general form of the figure is a spiral with ever-increasing lines extending out from *0* and forming ever decreasing angles. This is certainly a unique application of the famous Pythagorean theorem.

74

TRIANGULAR NUMBERS

THE NUMBERS 1, 3, 6, 10, 15, 21, 28, 36, 45, 55 are called triangular numbers because the units of which they are composed can be arranged in triangles, thus:

Note that each number is produced by adding $n + 1$ to the preceding number, where n is the number of the particular term: 21, for example, is obtained by adding $6 = (5 + 1)$ to 15, which is the fifth term of the series. Now if we multiply these triangular numbers by 6 each time and add 1 to the cube of k (where k represents the consecutive numbers 0, 1, 2, 3, 4, etc.) we get the cube of $k + 1$, thus:

$$
\begin{array}{cc}
k^3 & (k+1)^3 \\
(0 \times 6) + 1 + 0 = 1^3 \\
(1 \times 6) + 1 + 1 = 2^3 \\
(3 \times 6) + 1 + 8 = 3^3 \\
(6 \times 6) + 1 + 27 = 4^3 \\
(10 \times 6) + 1 + 64 = 5^3 \\
(15 \times 6) + 1 + 125 = 6^3 \\
(21 \times 6) + 1 + 216 = 7^3 \\
(28 \times 6) + 1 + 343 = 8^3
\end{array}
$$

Hence triangular numbers bear a definite relation to the series of cubes (third powers), just as the series of odd numbers bears a relation to the series of squares.

ODD SQUARES ALSO FORM A TRIANGLE

IT IS AN interesting fact that every odd square $(2n + 1)^2$ is the sum of $(2n + 1)$ consecutive integers beginning with $n + 1$. Thus:

$$1^2 = 1$$
$$3^2 = 2 + 3 + 4$$
$$5^2 = 3 + 4 + 5 + 6 + 7$$
$$7^2 = 4 + 5 + 6 + 7 + 8 + 9 + 10$$
$$9^2 = 5 + 6 + 7 + 8 + 9 + 10 + 11 + 12 + 13$$

· ·

CUBES, SQUARES AND TRIANGULAR NUMBERS

THE SUM of n terms of successive cubes, beginning with unity, turns out to be the square of the nth term of the triangular series (1 3 6 10 15 21 28 . . .). Thus, summing the successive cubes each time, to get the squares given in the second set of figures:

$1^3 =$	1	$1 =$	1^2
$2^3 =$	8	$9 =$	3^2
$3^3 =$	27	$36 =$	6^2
$4^3 =$	64	$100 =$	10^2
$5^3 =$	125	$225 =$	15^2
$6^3 =$	216	$441 =$	21^2
$7^3 =$	343	$784 =$	28^2
$8^3 =$	512	$1296 =$	36^2
$9^3 =$	729	$2025 =$	45^2
$10^3 =$	1000	$3025 =$	55^2

π, i, e AND LOGARITHMS

π, i and e are the most important constants in mathematics. π, of course, is the best known. Every elementary school student knows that it is the ratio of the circumference of a circle to the diameter and is equal to about 3.1416 or, roughly, 22/7.

But there are many other things that most people do not know about π. For one thing, it is not only irrational, so that its exact value can never be found no matter to how many places you figure it out, but it is also transcendental, which means that it is not the solution of any algebraic equation. Another thing that is not generally known about it is that it is the only constant of the three named here that was used by the ancients. Archimedes, who lived in the second century B.C., by using a regular polygon of 96 sides (for all practical purposes a circle), proved that the value of π was less than 22/7 and greater than 3 10/71, a remarkable achievement for the mathematics of his day. Ptolemy in A.D. 150 used the value of π as 3.1416 while the Chinese of that period jumped to the false conclusion that π was equal to the square root of 10 or 3.16227 ... In the middle of the sixteenth century the amazing fraction 355/113 was discovered, giving the value of π accurately to 6 decimal places. The actual value of π to 7 places is 3.1415926 ... and 355/113 equals 3.1415929 ...

Since the invention of the calculus and the discovery of infinite series the value of π can be calculated to any degree of accuracy that is desired. By extending the following series as far as we please we can "grind out" the value of π to any number of places in the decimals:

77

$$\frac{\pi}{6} = \frac{1}{2} + \left(\frac{1}{2}\right)\frac{1}{3}\left(\frac{1}{2}\right)^3 + \left(\frac{1}{2} \cdot \frac{3}{4}\right)\frac{1}{5}\left(\frac{1}{2}\right)^5 + \left(\frac{1}{2} \cdot \frac{3}{4} \cdot \frac{5}{6}\right)\frac{1}{7}\left(\frac{1}{2}\right)^7 + \cdots$$

By the early 17th century van Ceulen, a German mathematician, calculated π to more than 20 places and got 3.14159265-3589793238464 ... and it was worked out by man power to more than 700 places since that time. Our modern calculating machines have figured π to some 2000 places, which is more of a stunt than anything else. The textbook value of 3.1416 is good enough for ordinary computation.

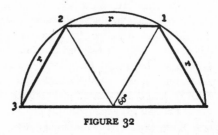

FIGURE 32

Figure 32 shows three equilateral triangles inside a semicircle. Of course each chord is equal to the radius of the circle since the triangles are equilateral, and you can see at once that the three chords cover the distance from one end of the semicircle to the other. In this case the three chords represent $3r$ where r is the radius of the circle. Now suppose you could push these three chords tight up against the circumference of the semicircle as shown in Figure 33. They will then lie along the curved line which is the semicircumference and, because they have been "pushed up" they will not make the entire distance from one end of the semicircle to the other as they did in Figure 32. There will then be a small arc AB left over which will equal .14159 ... or the decimal part of π. So the radius of the circle laid off on the semicircumference will go 3.14159 ... or π times. But the semicircumference equals 180 degrees so π must equal 180 degrees and 2π must equal 360 degrees, assuming a radius of 1 for the circle.

Now π equals 3.14159 . . . which represents 180 degrees. Hence 1 degree is π/180 or 3.1416/180 or .0174533. times the radius of

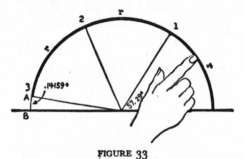

FIGURE 33

the circle. This is another very important constant as we shall see presently. Since π = 180°,

$$\pi/2 = 90°, \quad \pi/3 = 60°, \quad \pi/4 = 45°, \quad \pi/6 = 30°$$

This is a different way of expressing angles which is used almost exclusively in higher mathematics. Instead of reading an angle of 90° we read π/2; instead of 60° read π/3 and so on. Get in the habit of expressing the degrees of an angle in terms of π.

Figure 34 shows an ordinary protractor with the more important angles given in terms of π. The more familiar you become with it the better you will be able to understand some of the terms in higher mathematics.

Now look at Figure 33 again. Note that the angles of the triangles are no longer 60° but slightly less just as the length of the arc was. Instead of 60° the angle becomes 57° 17′ 44″ and this is called one *radian*. A radian is the number of degrees in an arc that is exactly equal to the radius of the circle; there are therefore 2π radians in the circle.

In Figure 35 we also see the radian value. Since 1° = .0174533,

1' must be 1/60 of this or .00029 and 1'' must be 1/60 of .00029 or .000005. Now it is a very simple matter to calculate the length

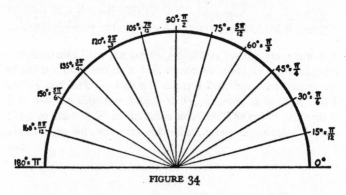

FIGURE 34

in feet and inches of any arc if we know the radius of the circle and the number of degrees in the arc. Just multiply the radius by the number of degrees and multiply the result by .0174533 plus the constants for the minutes and seconds. Suppose we want to

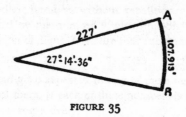

FIGURE 35

find the length of the arc *AB* in Figure 35 in feet and inches. We go about it as follows:

Arc	27°	14'	36''	27 × .01745	.47115
				14 × .00029	.00406
				36 × .000005	.00018
					.47539

This .47539 is the length of the arc in feet for a radius of 1. But the radius of our circle is 227 feet so we multiply this by 227 and get the length of arc *AB* as 107.913 feet.

The radius of the earth is 3963 miles, so one degree of latitude on the earth's surface is .0174533 × 3963 miles, or 69.41 miles. Degrees of longitude vary, since all longitude lines converge to the poles. A nautical mile is really one minute of latitudinal arc on the earth's surface, or 1/60 of 69.41 miles, and a knot is a nautical mile per hour. When a ship makes 40 knots it is traveling 40 nautical miles per hour and covering 40 minutes of arc on the earth's surface every hour.

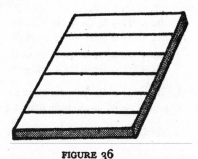

FIGURE 36

It is a remarkable fact that π pops up in the laws of chance. This has been demonstrated many times by means of a sheet of cardboard, with parallel lines on it, and a needle (Figure 36). The parallel lines are spaced twice the length of the needle apart and the needle is tossed into the air and allowed to fall anyway on the sheet. The object of this test is to determine the relation between the number of tosses of the needle and the number of times the needle touches any line. Count Buffon, in the eighteenth century, made this test himself and found that the relation mentioned came closer and closer to 3.1416 as the number of tosses increased. In 1901 a scientist made 3400 tosses of the needle and found that it touched a line 1082 times. This ratio, 3400/1082, differs from π by less than one-tenth of one percent.

Assuming that the number of touches of the needle to a line is proportional to the length of the needle we can get some idea why π figures in this experiment of pure chance. Suppose the needle were not straight but circular. And further suppose that the circumference of this circular needle were 2π times the length of the original needle or, in other words, the radius of the circular needle is equal to the length of the original needle. Then the number of times this circular needle will touch a line will always be two times the number of tosses. This is because a line always cuts a circle in two parts and also because the lines are spaced twice the length of the needle or twice the radius of the circular needle. So no matter where the circular needle fell it must touch two lines—it can never touch no lines. But the circumference of this circular needle is 2π times the regular needle and the number of times it crosses a line is always twice the number of times it is tossed, hence: $2\pi C = 2T$ where C is crossings and T is tosses. From this we get $\pi = T/C$.

$\overset{\bullet}{i}$

You don't have to be a mathematician to know that $\sqrt{4} = \pm 2$ or the $\sqrt{36} = \pm 6$. Every youngster in elementary school knows the simpler square roots of numbers that are squares. And every elementary-school student knows that a minus times a minus is a plus. A double negative is poor English because it does not convey the meaning you want it to convey. If you say "I don't have no time to do this" you are really saying, "I have time to do this" because the two negatives, "don't" and "no" form an affirmative.

An excellent visual example of two negatives making a positive is shown in many drug stores. The bromo-seltzer bottle in order to dispense the powder is always upside down, yet the label on it is right side up. If right side up is $+$ and upside down is $-$, then the label was put on the bottle upside down when the bottle was right side up. We start with a minus on the label. Now we turn the bottle upside down and in so doing cause the bottle to go through a "minus" which doubles the "minus" of the label and we get it right side up or +.

So we can say that $\sqrt{4}$ = +2 and −2 and the $\sqrt{36}$ = +6 and −6 and we find that there is no number which, when multiplied by itself, will be a minus number. Now the question is: does the square root of a negative number actually exist? Is there any such number as $\sqrt{-1}$ or $\sqrt{-7}$ or $\sqrt{-236}$? These symbols indicate numbers that, when squared, give negative numbers. Are there such numbers? Yes, there are; but these numbers are not real in the same sense that 7 and 18 and 45 are real. They are called *imaginary* and are designated by the small letter *i*. Thus *i* is the square root of minus 1 ($i = \sqrt{-1}$), and any number times *i* is the same as the square root of its negative. Thus 6*i* is the same as $\sqrt{-36}$, 3*i* is the same as $\sqrt{-9}$ and so on.

But, while *i* itself is not real and exists in the imagination, the even powers of *i* are very real and extremely important as we shall see presently. The powers of *i* are:

$$i = \sqrt{-1}$$
$$i^2 = -1$$
$$i^3 = -\sqrt{-1}$$
$$i^4 = +1$$

All even powers of *i* are either −1 or +1 and whenever you see i^2 you can be sure that it is −1, while i^4 is +1 and so on. It follows from this that $8i^2$ is −8 and $29i^4$ is + 29, and so on. These imaginary numbers, which appeared at first to exist only in the imagination and to have no real significance, actually transform themselves into real numbers when raised to even powers.

A most fascinating discovery was that every number has *n* *n*th roots: 7, for example, has 3 cube roots, 5 fifth roots, and so on; and so has 16, for any number at all has *n* *n*th roots. Maybe this is not news to you, but ask anyone you know (provided he is not a mathematician) what the cube root of 8 is. He will say "2" just like that. But he is only one third correct. There are two other cube roots of 8 and, while we can't conceive them since they are what we call *complex* numbers, they exist nevertheless. This is extremely interesting. Here are two inconceivable numbers that we can't use at all, yet if either of them is cubed it will give the answer of 8. To prove this let us examine the three cube roots of 8. They are: 2, $-1 + i\sqrt{3}$ and $-1 - i\sqrt{3}$. Let us cube this $-1 + i\sqrt{3}$ and see if it actually gives us 8. Remember that $i^2 = -1$ and $3i^2 = -3$.

$$
\begin{array}{r}
-1 + i\sqrt{3} \\
-1 + i\sqrt{3} \\
\hline
+1 - i\sqrt{3} \\
- i\sqrt{3} - 3 \\
\hline
-2 - 2i\sqrt{3}
\end{array}
\qquad (i\sqrt{3}^2 = 3i^2 = -3)
$$

Now
$$
\begin{array}{r}
-2 - 2i\sqrt{3} \\
-1 + i\sqrt{3} \\
\hline
+2 + 2i\sqrt{3} \\
- 2i\sqrt{3} - (-6) \\
\hline
+2 \qquad +6 \\
2 + 6 = 8
\end{array}
\qquad (-2 \times 3i^2 = -2 \times -3 = +6)
$$

So we see that the cube of $-1 + i\sqrt{3}$, which is a complex number or the combination of a real and an imaginary number, actually turns out to be 8. The same result would be obtained if we cubed the other complex number $-1 - i\sqrt{3}$. So 8 has three cube roots, one real and two imaginary.

In the same way there are five fifth roots of 32, ten tenth roots of 1024 and so on. Every number has n nth roots; but in every case the maximum number of real roots—composed of numbers that we use every day—is two regardless of how many roots the number has.

This is beautifully shown and explained by graphic representation. Figure 37 shows the regular X and Y axis so familiar to all who work with graphs. Let us call the $+1$ on the X axis B and the -1 on the X axis A. Let us also call the $+1$ on the Y axis P. If we now join A and B to P forming two equal right triangles, we have the well known relation: $OA : OP = OP : OB$ because angle APB is a right angle and all the triangles are similar. It follows from this that $OP^2 = OA \times OB$ or $OP^2 = +1 \times -1 = -1$.

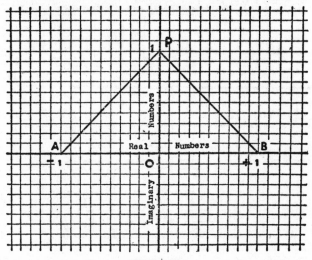

FIGURE 37

This being the case, OP must represent $\sqrt{-1}$ or i. In the same way the point 2 on the Y axis is $2\sqrt{-1}$ or $2i$ and 3 is $3i$ and so on. So the Y axis becomes the axis of imaginaries. Above the X axis all imaginaries are $+$; below the X axis all imaginaries are $-$.

Any point on the Y axis gives us an imaginary number and any point on the X axis gives us a real number. What about all the numbers that are on neither axis? These numbers are real plus imaginary numbers and are called *complex* numbers. They are all of the form $x + iy$. These complex numbers are plotted just as other numbers are in graphic work. $5 + 3i$ for example, is $+5$ on the X axis and 3 up on the Y axis as shown by the point R in Figure 38.

Now let us go back to the three cube roots of 8 and plot them on our new graph. The square root of 3 is 1.73 . . . so $-1 + \sqrt{3}$ is found 1 to the left of the Y axis and 1.73 up and $-1 - \sqrt{3}$ is found 1 to the left of the Y axis and 1.73 down as shown on the

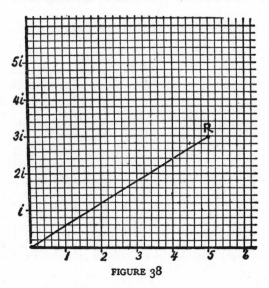

FIGURE 38

diagram Figure 39. The third root of 2, of course, is $+2$ and if all the points are joined we get an equilateral triangle showing the three cube roots of 8 graphically.

Just as the three cube roots of any number are represented by an equilateral triangle, so the four fourth roots form a square, the five fifth roots a pentagon, the six sixth roots a hexagon and so on. In every case the maximum number of real roots is never greater than two since real roots are shown *only* on the X axis. Figure 40 shows a pentagon which gives us the five fifth roots of 32. These roots are:

$+2$, $-1.618 + 1.175i$, $-1.618 - 1.175i$, $.618 + 1.9i$ and $.618 - 1.9i$.

If you multiply any or all of these five fifth roots of 32 by themselves five times you will get 32 in each case.

By graphic means you can compute to a fair degree of accuracy the *n* *n*th roots of any number at all. It is just a question of the

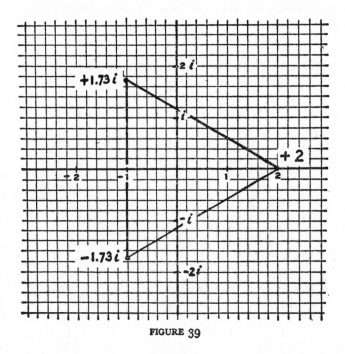

FIGURE 39

type of regular polygon to build on the *X* axis; the number of sides of the polygon is the same as the number of roots of the number you wish to find. The three cube roots form a triangle, the four fourth roots form a square, the five fifth roots a pentagon, the six sixth roots a hexagon, and so on. All these figures are regular polygons whose vertices give the real and imaginary roots of the given number. Since we always start on the positive real

X axis, all even number roots form regular polygons with an even number of sides and consequently there are always two *real* roots, one + and one — All odd number roots form regular polygons with an odd number of sides and so there are no real negative roots, as you can see from the two diagrams Figures 39 and 40.

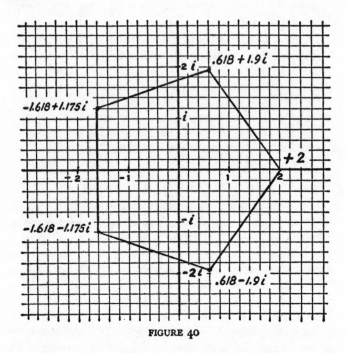

FIGURE 40

It's fun to compute the n nth roots of a number accurately and know that all the "spooky" imaginary roots actually spring to reality when multiplied sufficiently by themselves. If you are familiar with elementary trigonometry you can apply the following formula, which may look complicated but is in reality very simple:

$$^{n}\sqrt{x} = x^{\frac{1}{n}}\left[\cos\frac{2k\pi}{n} + i\sin\frac{2k\pi}{n}\right]$$

where $x^{\frac{1}{n}}$ is the ordinary root $\left(32^{\frac{1}{5}} = 2\right)$

All you need do is substitute the root for n and use k as 0, 1, 2, 3, 4, etc., according to how much n is; π, of course, is 180°. Here is the way it works for the five fifth roots of 32. Here x is 32, n is 5 and k will be 0, 1, 2, 3 and 4. When k is 0 this formula becomes:

$$2\ [\cos 0° + i\sin 0°]$$

since $\cos 0° = 1$ and $\sin 0° = 0$ this becomes simply 2, which is the only real root. So one of the five fifth roots of 32 is 2. Now let $k = 1$ and this formula becomes:

$$2\left[\cos\frac{2\pi}{5} + i\sin\frac{2\pi}{5}\right]$$

Cos $2\pi/5$ equals cos 360°/5 or cos 72°. We then have:

$$2\ [\cos 72° + i\sin 72°]$$

and by reference to sine and cosine tables we get:

$$2\ [.3090 + 9511\ i],$$

which gives us $.618 + 1.9022\ i$. So we see that $.618 + 1.9022\ i$ is another one of the five fifth roots of 32 and if this is multiplied by itself five times the result will be 32.

The same procedure applies for the other three roots when $k = 2$, $k = 3$, and $k = 4$. By applying this formula you can get all the n nth roots of any number you choose, and when graphed they will all lie in a regular polygon with n sides. If n is even, there will be two real roots on the X axis; if n is odd, there will be only one real root on the X axis. In any event you can be sure that the polygons will be regular and once you know the root you can plot the polygon since the five fifth roots will be a pentagon, the six sixth roots will be a hexagon, the seven seventh roots a heptagon and so on.

So, out of the mind of man comes a number that in itself is impossible to conceive, a number that for all practical purposes does not exist in the same sense that positive and negative numbers exist. Yet this imaginary number, $\sqrt{-1}$ or i, plays a vital part in higher mathematics, physics and, particularly, theoretical electricity.

e AND LOGARITHMS

THE THIRD vitally important constant in our trio is designated by the small letter e, which is the initial letter in the word *exponential*. This constant, like π, is both irrational and transcendental. It was first derived by John Napier, the inventor of logarithms, to whom we owe an everlasting debt of gratitude. If e had never been discovered, mathematics, astronomy and physics would be put back a century or more, because e is the base of all natural logarithms and logarithms play an enormously important role in mathematics and science.

The constant e is the limiting value of the fraction $\left(1 + \dfrac{1}{n}\right)^n$ as n approaches infinity. Its exact value can never be found, but to 15 places it is 2.718281828459045 . . . Let us see how this is arrived at. Let us first take $1\frac{1}{2}$ and square it; we get $2\frac{1}{4}$. If we cube 1 1/3 we get 2.3686. If we raise $1\frac{1}{4}$ to the fourth power we get 2.4414 and, in general, as n increases in the fraction $\left(1 + \dfrac{1}{n}\right)^n$ we get nearer and nearer to this 2.71828 . . .

$$\left(1 + \frac{1}{2}\right)^2 = 2.2500 \qquad \left(1 + \frac{1}{10}\right)^{10} = 2.5940$$

$$\left(1 + \frac{1}{3}\right)^3 = 2.3686 \qquad \left(1 + \frac{1}{100}\right)^{100} = 2.7051$$

$$\left(1 + \frac{1}{4}\right)^4 = 2.4414 \qquad \left(1 + \frac{1}{1000}\right)^{1000} = 2.7180$$

The value of e may be found to as many places as desired by expanding the fraction $\left(1 + \dfrac{1}{n}\right)^n$ by the binomial theorem and letting n approach infinity. By doing this we get:

$$e = 1 + 1 + \frac{1}{2!} + \frac{1}{3!} + \frac{1}{4!} + \frac{1}{5!} \cdots \frac{1}{n!}$$

and if we expand $\left(1 + \dfrac{1}{n}\right)^{nx}$ we get

$$e^x = 1 + x + \frac{x^2}{2!} + \frac{x^3}{3!} + \frac{x^4}{4!} + \frac{x^5}{5!} \cdots \frac{x^n}{n!}$$

This series means that we can put any exponent we want for x and can "grind out" its value.

You can readily see that, since $2! = 1 \times 2$, $3! = 1 \times 2 \times 3$, $4! = 1 \times 2 \times 3 \times 4$, and so on, we get

$$e = 1 + 1 + \frac{1}{2} + \frac{1}{6} + \frac{1}{24} + \frac{1}{120} + \cdots$$

and this equals:

$$
\begin{array}{l}
2.000000 \\
.500000 \\
.166667 \\
.041667 \\
\underline{.008333} \\
2.716667 \ldots
\end{array}
$$

If carried out to five more places we would get $2.718281 \ldots = e$

So in e^x we have a sort of mathematical machine where we can "put in" anything we like for x, "turn the crank" and out comes the value all done for us. Just to get used to this idea let us take a few strange exponents and put them in the e^x series;

$$e^{\sin \theta} = 1 + \sin \theta + \frac{\sin^2 \theta}{2!} + \frac{\sin^3 \theta}{3!} + \frac{\sin^4 \theta}{4!} \cdots \frac{\sin^n \theta}{n!}$$

$$e^i = 1 + i + \frac{i^2}{2!} + \frac{i^3}{3!} + \frac{i^4}{4!} + \cdots \frac{i^n}{n!}$$

$$e^{\text{anything}} = 1 + \text{anything} + \frac{\text{anything}^2}{2!} + \frac{\text{anything}^3}{3!} + \frac{\text{anything}^4}{4!} \cdots$$

So far we have shown some interesting properties of e but as yet we have not attempted to explain just why it is solely responsible for such a priceless mathematical treasure as logarithms. The constant e is known as the Napierian base of natural logarithms and, in order to understand why, we must know something about the nature of logarithms.

A logarithm is defined as "the exponent of that power of a fixed number, called the base, which equals a given number." For example:

$$4^3 = 64; \text{ so 3 is the logarithm of } 64 \text{ to the base } 4$$
$$5^2 = 25; \text{ so 2 is the logarithm of } 25 \text{ to the base } 5$$
$$10^2 = 100; \text{ so 2 is the logarithm of } 100 \text{ to the base } 10$$

and, in general, if $B^x = N$, then x is the logarithm of N to the base B.

You can see at once how different this is from an ordinary algebraic function. If $y = x^2$, then x must equal $\sqrt{y}$ and if $u = v^3$ then $v = \sqrt[3]{u}$. The inverse of these algebraic functions is simple and can easily be found because the exponent is a constant: 2, 3, 4, or any other number, never varies. But if we have the function $y = 2^x$ where x varies, we can't say that 2 is the xth root of y because that is not what we want. We then say that x is the logarithm of y to the base 2. The word *logarithm* is abbreviated to log and the base (when shown) is always written a little below thus: $\log_{10}$. So we write:

$$\text{If } 6^2 = 36, \text{ then } 2 = \log_6 36,$$
$$\text{If } 10^3 = 1000 \text{ then } 3 = \log_{10} 1000,$$
$$\text{If } e^k = 14 \text{ then } k = \log_e 14 \ldots.$$

See the two columns, A and B on page 95. Obviously the nth term of the numbers in A is n and the nth term of the numbers in B is 3^n. Now let $y = 3^n$. Then, by definition, $n = \log_3 y$. But $y = 3^n$, hence the numbers in column A are the logarithms of those in column B to the base 3. Now multiply any two numbers in column B as follows: add the numbers in column A opposite them and look in column *B* for the answer. Take 27 × 729. Opposite 27 we see 3; opposite 729 we see 6: 3 + 6 = 9. Opposite 9 read 19683 in the *B* column. This is the product of 27 and 729.

The reverse also holds true. To divide, just subtract the numbers opposite. To divide 6561 by 243 subtract 5 from 8 and get 3. Now look opposite 3 and get 27. This shows that two numbers are multiplied by adding their logarithms, and that one number is divided into another by subtracting its logarithm from the logarithm of the other.

The logarithms that we use in practical work like engineering, surveying and astronomy are to the base 10 because that is just as simple as the decimal system is in arithmetic. In this base, log 10 is 1, log 100 is 2, log 1000 is 3, log 10,000 is 4 and so on, since $10^1 = 10$, $10^2 = 100$, $10^3 = 1000$ and $10^4 = 10,000$. All logs of numbers between 1 and 10 are between 0 and 1, all logs of numbers between 10 and 100 are between 1 and 2, all logs of numbers between 100 and 1000 are between 2 and 3, and so on.

Take a number like 20. Its logarithm lies between 1 and 2 and, from the table in the back of the book we see that it is 1.30103. This means that $10^{1.30103} = 20$. Notice that the log of 2 is also .30103 without the 1 in front. The reason is obvious: 20 is 10 times 2 and when we multiply by 10 we add the log of 10 which is 1. In the same way 200 would be 2.30103 and 2000 would be 3.30103. The decimal part of the logarithm, which is called the *mantissa*, always remains the same for any given number and the whole number, called the *characteristic*, changes only with the multiples of 10. In looking up logs, you will find only the mantissa given and it is up to you to supply the whole number. The mantissa of the log of 31 is the same as that of 3.1 or 310 or 3100 or 31000; it only remains to precede the mantissa by the proper characteristic, thus: log 31 = 1.49136, log 3.1 = .49136, log 310 = 2.49136, log 3100 = 3.49136, etc.

Now you can amuse yourself by multiplying numbers by adding their logarithms. Look up their logs, add these logs and look up the result. From the table in the back of the book, log 16 = 1.20412 and log 3 = .47712. Adding these two logs we get 1.68124. Looking in the log column for 68124 we find it opposite 48. So 16 × 3 = 48. You can multiply two, three, four or any number of numbers together quickly merely by adding up their logs and referring to that log in the table. The same idea in reverse applies to division. Just look up the logs of the two numbers, subtract one log from the other and find the number corresponding with the result.

Just as adding the logs of numbers multiplies these numbers, so raising a number to a given power is accomplished by multiplying the log of that number by that power and looking up the number corresponding to that result. To take a few examples: $3^4 = 4 \log 3$, and the number corresponding to this is the answer: $4 \times \log 3$ is $4 \times .47712 = 1.90848$. Now look for this 1.90848 in the table and see 81 opposite it. So $3^4 = 81$. In the same way $6^2 = 2 \times \log 6$ or $2 \times .77815 = 1.55630$. Looking up 1.55630 we get 36. The reverse is also true. To get any root of a number divide its log by that root and find the number corresponding to the result in the table.

So, tedious multiplications and divisions become simple addition and subtraction in logarithmic work and raising to any power and taking any root become simple multiplication and division. You can see at once how this simplifies work and saves hours of time. Think how long it would take you to find the value of the following without the use of logs:

$$\frac{185764^4 \times 97623^5}{169 \times 86593 \times 47^2} \qquad \frac{365^{1.45} \times \sqrt[4]{197}}{\sqrt{564^4 \times 45^3}}$$

So we can put down the four fundamental rules in using logarithms:

1. $\log (A \times B)$ = $\log A + \log B$
2. $\log (A/B)$ = $\log A - \log B$
3. $\log (A^n)$ = n times $\log A$
4. $\log (\sqrt[n]{A})$ = $\log A$ divided by n

The log table in the back of the book gives logs from 1 to 100.

Practice using them. Note that the mantessa is the same for any multiple of 10, like 20, 200, 2000.

Now, to get back to our friend e and how these log tables came into existence. Of all bases to select, why do we take the base e which is 2.71828 . . . ? Isn't this rather foolish when we can use 10 so easily as a base? Why is this e so important and how did it play such a vital role in the invention of logarithms?

To answer this question completely and thoroughly is far beyond the scope of this book and needs a knowledge and familiarity with the processes of differentiation and integration in the calculus. But you can get some idea, some "bird's eye view" of the general reason, if you consider that all logs are the result of a series somewhat like the e^x series. The simplest log series is:

A	B
1	3
2	9
3	27
4	81
5	243
6	729
7	2187
8	6561
9	19683
10	59049
11	177147
12	531441

$$\text{Log}_e (1 + x) = x - \frac{x^2}{2} + \frac{x^3}{3} - \frac{x^4}{4} + \frac{x^5}{5} \ldots \pm \frac{x^n}{n}$$

If you substitute 1 for x you get log 2; if you substitute 2 for x you get log 3. It is all a question of putting the value of x in this long chain of numbers and adding and subtracting as directed. This is the simplest log series but it is by no means the best, for it would take a thousand terms of adding and subtracting to get the value of a log correct to only three decimal places. A much more elaborate series has been devised which gives the logs quickly. The important thing to remember is not so much the type of elaborate series that we use to "grind out" logs, but the *fundamental basis* of it all. The simple but impractical series shown here gave rise to the more elaborate one, so it has a very important place in the general scheme. But how do we get this $\log_e (1 + x)$ series and why is it to the base e instead of the base 10?

The fundamental facts are very simple even if the methods are involved and rather complicated. It all boils down to this:

95

1. Logarithms can be determined to any number of places only by means of an elaborate infinite series which has for its basis the simple series mentioned above, namely:

$$\text{Log}_e (1 + x) = x - \frac{x^2}{2} + \frac{x^3}{3} - \frac{x^4}{4} + \frac{x^5}{5} \ldots$$

2. This very simple series was evolved by dividing $1 + x$ into 1, giving:

$$\frac{1}{1 + x} = 1 - x + x^2 - x^3 + x^4 - x^5 \ldots$$

After this is done the series is integrated by methods of the integral calculus (with which we do not need to concern ourselves in this book), and we get:

$$\log_e (1 + x) = x - \frac{x^2}{2} + \frac{x^3}{3} - \frac{x^4}{4} + \frac{x^5}{5} - \frac{x^6}{6} \ldots$$

which is the series already mentioned.

3. Integration is a process which is just the reverse of differentiation, and it is in differentiation that e plays such a vital role. A logarithm to any base whatsoever cannot possibly be differentiated without this already familiar fraction: $\left(1 + \frac{1}{n}\right)^n$. Look on page 176 in the back of the book and see the differentiation of $\text{Log}_e x$. There is no need to try to understand the method. What is important is to recognize this fraction $\left(1 + \frac{1}{n}\right)^n$, which takes the form $\left(1 + \frac{\triangle x}{x}\right)^{\frac{x}{\triangle x}}$ and which, when x approaches infinity, becomes nearer and nearer equal to e or 2.71828 . . .

4. So, without this $\left(1 + \frac{\triangle x}{x}\right)^{\frac{x}{\triangle x}}$ which is used to get the base e, we could not hope to differentiate any logarithm. Without being able to differentiate a logarithm we could not integrate the simple series:

$$1 - x + x^2 - x^3 + x^4 - x^5 \ldots$$

and without integrating this simple series we could not get the series:

$$\log_e (1 + x) = x - \frac{x^2}{2} + \frac{x^3}{3} - \frac{x^4}{4} \cdots$$

on which the entire structure of logarithms (to the base *e*) is built.

So all our logarithms, to any base whatever, are calculated from the complicated series evolved from $\log_e (1 + x)$, and would therefore be impossible if it were not for *e*. That is why *e* is so important to us, and why it is the base of all natural logarithms used in higher mathematics.

All natural logs can be easily converted into logarithms to the base 10 (called Briggs or common logarithms) by multiplying them by .4342 . . . The natural logarithm of 2 (to the base *e*) is .6931471 . . . which, when multiplied by .4342 . . . gives .3010300, the log of 2 to the base 10.

The common logarithms that we use in engineering, surveying and astronomy were calculated from the natural logarithms (to the base *e*) by Henry Briggs, professor of geometry in Gresham College, London, in the year 1615, and the first table of common logarithms to appear anywhere was published by a colleague of Briggs named Gunter in 1620. Today we can get log tables to ten or more places. Such tables are of indescribable value in physics and astronomy.

In his book, *Mathematics, Its Magic and Mastery*, Dr. Aaron Bakst shows an ingenious way to calculate common logs to three decimal places. All that is necessary, of course, are the logs of prime numbers since all the other logs may be obtained by adding. $\log_{10} 2$ in Dr. Bakst's method is as follows:

> $2^{10} = 1024$. We don't know the log of 1024 but we do know the log of 1000 which is 3. If $2^{10} = 3$, then, by definition, $10 \log 2 = 3$, or $\log 2 = .3$. Now the error is .0024 since we have 1024 and not 1000, so we make the correction by adding

.3 × .0024 or .0007, which we can call .001. Hence the log of 2 by this method is .301, and this is correct to three places.

In the same way log 3 can be found by the fact that $3^4 = 81$. Taking 80 instead of 81 we get: $3^4 = 80$ or 10×2^3. But this can be expressed as $3 \times \log 2 + \log 10$, or $3 \times .301 + 1$, which is 1.903. 3^4 therefore is equal to 1.903, so log 3 = 1.903/4 which is .476. Again allowing for the error of 1 in 81 we get log 3 = .477. From these two logs we can get logs 4, 5, (log 5 = 1 − log 2) 6, 8 and 9. All these can be found by addition or, in the case of 5, by subtraction. Log 7 is found by the fact that $7^4 = 2401$. Calling 2400 8 × 3 × 100, we just add log 8, log 3 and log 100, all of which we have calculated already. This comes to .903 + .477 + 2 or 3.380. Then 4 × log 7 equals 3.380 or log 7 = .845.

Dr. Bakst gives similar methods for calculating other prime logs up to 100 and, while his system is unique and simple, it is nevertheless limited to logs of three places. The only way to find logarithms to any high degree of accuracy is by means of the complicated series we have been discussing. Patient, lifelong work on the part of men like Briggs and Gunter have given us the priceless logarithm tables, figured to ten or more decimal places, without which astronomy and other mathematical sciences would suffer enormously.

The Sine and Cosine Tables

The constant e also plays an important role in the derivation of the tables of natural sines and cosines so vital to the engineer, architect, navigator, surveyor and physicist. This time it is not only e that takes a bow but our friend i, the imaginary number, the square root of minus 1. These two amazing constants help to build the very real and practical sine and cosine tables. To understand how they do it, let us go back to our e^x series. We said that x can be anything we like, so let us make it equal to $i\theta$, where θ is any angle. We then have:

$$e^{i\theta} = 1 + i\theta + \frac{i^2\theta^2}{2!} + \frac{i^3\theta^3}{3!} + \frac{i^4\theta^4}{4!} + \frac{i^5\theta^5}{5}$$

Leonhard Euler, a great Swiss mathematician in the middle of the eighteenth century, proved that $e^{i\theta} = \cos\theta + i\sin\theta$, and from this great discovery we can build up the tables of sines and cosines simply by putting:

$$e^{i\theta} = 1 + i\theta - \frac{\theta^2}{2!} - \frac{i\theta^3}{3!} + \frac{\theta^4}{4!} + \frac{i\theta^5}{5!} \ldots \text{ (note that } i^2 = -1 \text{ and } i^3 = -i)$$

Take particular notice that some of the terms have i in them and some are without i. All the terms with i in them belong to the *sine* series, and all those without the i belong to the *cosine* series, since Euler's formula distinctly states $e^{i\theta} = \cos\theta + i\sin\theta$. Hence:

$$e^{i\theta} = \underbrace{1 - \frac{\theta^2}{2!} + \frac{\theta^4}{4!} - \frac{\theta^6}{6!} \ldots}_{\cos\theta} + i \underbrace{\left[\theta - \frac{\theta^3}{3!} + \frac{\theta^5}{5!} - \frac{\theta^7}{7} \ldots \right]}_{\sin\theta}$$

So

$$\cos\theta = 1 - \frac{\theta^2}{2!} + \frac{\theta^4}{4!} - \frac{\theta^6}{6!} \ldots$$

$$\sin\theta = \theta - \frac{\theta^3}{3!} + \frac{\theta^5}{5!} - \frac{\theta^7}{7!} \ldots$$

where θ is in radian measure, which we discussed in the section on π.

So out of these three remarkable constants, two of which are irrational and transcendental and the other imaginary, we get the logarithm and trigonometric tables and a great many other valuable mathematical concepts which have helped to advance our scientific knowledge and give us such inventions as radio, television, the telephone and hundreds of other amazing electrical instruments.

Perhaps the most amazing of all formulas in mathematics is the famous formula of Euler, which is $e^{i\pi} = -1$. This connects four of the most important constants of mathematics in a single formula, as can be seen if we substitute π for θ in the formula above: $e^{i\pi} = \cos\pi + i\sin\pi = -1$.

THE WONDERS OF THE NOMOGRAPH

A NOMOGRAPH is a diagram that enables anyone, with the aid of a straightedge, to read off the value of a desired quantity, called the dependent variable, when the value of another quantity, called the independent variable, is given.

The subject of nomography is a comparatively recent one dating back to the middle of the last century. The man most responsible for the development of the subject is M. d'Ocagne, and most of the works on the subject are in French.

Nomographs save hours of concentrated calculation and tedious work. Solely by connecting two vertical lines with a straightedge one can instantly solve difficult and complicated problems in physics and engineering. Engineering problems in water pressure, fluid velocity, pipe flow, maximum moment, column loads, beam stress, belt design, gas expansion, boiler efficiency, voltage drop, power factor, capacitance and thousands of others become as simple as measuring a line with a ruler. Here, for example, is one of the complicated formulas in engineering solved very quickly for P_1 and P_2 by means of a straightedge and a nomograph:

$$\frac{P_2}{P_1} = \left(\frac{2y}{y+1} \right) M_1{}^2 \sin^2 \theta_w - \left(\frac{y-1}{y+1} \right)$$

Generally any line or graph which will solve an equation directly or translate one system into another can be classed as a nomograph. In Figure 41, for example, we have a very simple nomograph—a line which shows two scales: the bottom scale in inches and the top scale in centimeters. We change one system into another merely by comparing one scale with another.

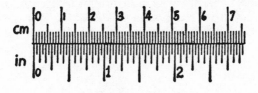

FIGURE 41

Figure 42 shows a circular slide rule and gives, by direct reading, the squares and cubes of numbers as well as their square and cube roots. Take any number on the *A* or *B* scale, join it with a straightedge to the center and you will find its cube directly above it and its square directly below it. Suppose you take 5 and join it

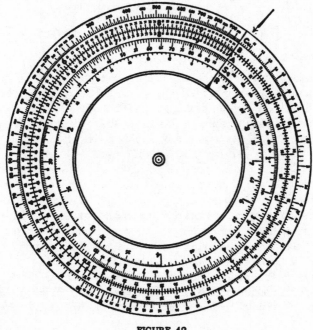

FIGURE 42

to the center. Directly above the 5 the straightedge shows the cube of 5 which is 125 (halfway between 120 and 130, each space representing two units). Directly below the 5 read the square of 5 which is 25. You can do the same with any other number on the *A* or *B*

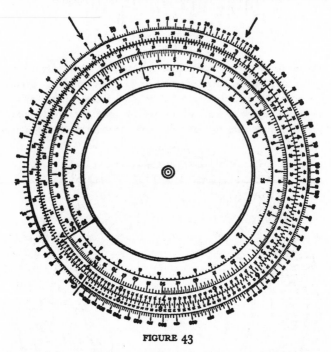

FIGURE 43

scale and get its cube or its square by referring to the scale directly above or below. After you have played around with this a little, reversing the process to get square roots and cube roots, look at the *R* scale, which is the innermost circle. This gives decimal equivalents. This is nothing more than the reverse scale we discuss in the section on how to make a slide rule from a ruler. Treating each one of these numbers as a reciprocal, we see that 1/6 when referred back to the A or B scale is .167. The 4 on the R scale, expressed as $\frac{1}{4}$, becomes .25 when referred back to the A or B scales. And so it is for all the other numbers.

In the actual slide rule the cube scale Cu and B scale remain stationary, while the wheel with the other 3 scales A, S and R, rotates. Now, when π on the square scale is directly under 2 on the B scale as shown in Figure 43, all numbers on the B scale become diameters of circles while all numbers on the square scale become the areas. For example, a circle with a diameter of 3 has an area of 7.1. It's as simple as that! By setting 2 on the A scale directly under the V on the cube scale, furthermore, the numbers on the A scale become diameters of spheres and those on the cube scale give the volumes. A sphere with a diameter of 4 has a volume of 33.3. And so it is with hundreds of other settings and readings—just as quick and just as simple!

There is plenty of interesting and valuable mathematical information in these diagrams and the longer you play around with them the more you will discover. In a sense they may be called nomographs since they compare one scale with another. The typical nomograph consists of two graduated vertical lines with a line or curve midway between them. They all make use of a straightedge and the construction of simple nomographs is ridiculously easy. In Figure 44, which is an addition nomograph, you see three vertical lines lettered at the bottom A, C, and B. The line C is exactly the same distance from A as it is from B. Lines A and B are numbered in even spaces above and below the horizontal line which represents zero. All the numbers above are positive or plus, all the numbers below are negative or minus. The center line C is also numbered above and below the zero, but you will note that there are two spaces for one on the A or B. The line C then has just twice as many numbers as the lines A and B. Now take a straightedge and connect any number on A with any number on B and you will find their sum where that line crosses the center line C. If you connect 6 with 8, for example, your straightedge will

A + B = C

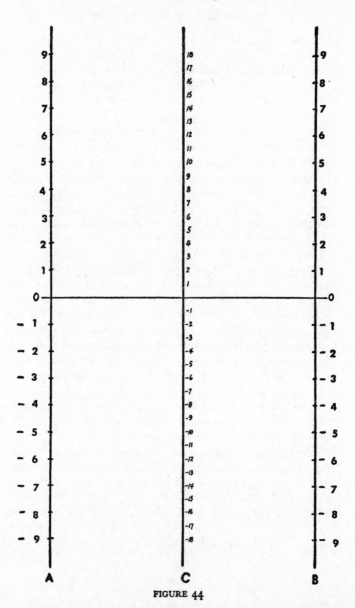

FIGURE 44

cut C at 14. Connect 9 on A with -5 on B and you will see that the straightedge cuts the line C at 4. Connecting -6 on A with $+1$ on B the straightedge cûts -5 on B.

In subtracting negative numbers we get positive results. Thus $6 - (-2)$ gives $+8$. Join 6 on the C line to -2 on the A line and extend it to the B line. So you can see this is a regular adding machine which never makes a mistake. $A + B$ always equals C. In the same way $A - C$ will equal B, as you can verify with the straightedge.

In Figure 45 we have essentially the same nomograph, the three vertical lines or columns, but this time we multiply instead of adding or subtracting. Here the product of A and B always equals C. The vertical lines A and B, instead of being divided equally as they were in Figure 44, are divided, so that they form two vertical and equal slide-rule scales. The line C, exactly half way between A and B, is divided into twice as many parts, just as the line C was in the addition nomograph. Now take your straightedge and connect any number on A with any number on B. If you hold the straightedge horizontally connecting 5 with 5 or 3 with 3, it will give you the squares of these numbers when it crosses C. If therefore you wish to get the squares of any of the numbers on A or B, connect the same numbers on both scales, and note where it intersects the center of C. Now suppose you want to multiply 2×4. It makes no difference whether you start on A or B: the straightedge will always cross C at 8. So if you connect any number on either outside scale with any number on the other scale, the product will always be found on the middle scale C. Obviously division may be performed just as easily: 20 divided by 4, for example, merely means connecting 4 on A with the 20 on C and extending it until you come to 5 on B.

One of the most interesting and amazing nomographs is shown in Figure 46. As you can see by the equation it instantly gives you powers and roots of numbers. If you know x and n you can instantly get y. And the beauty of it is that without the use of logarithms it gives you decimal powers and roots.

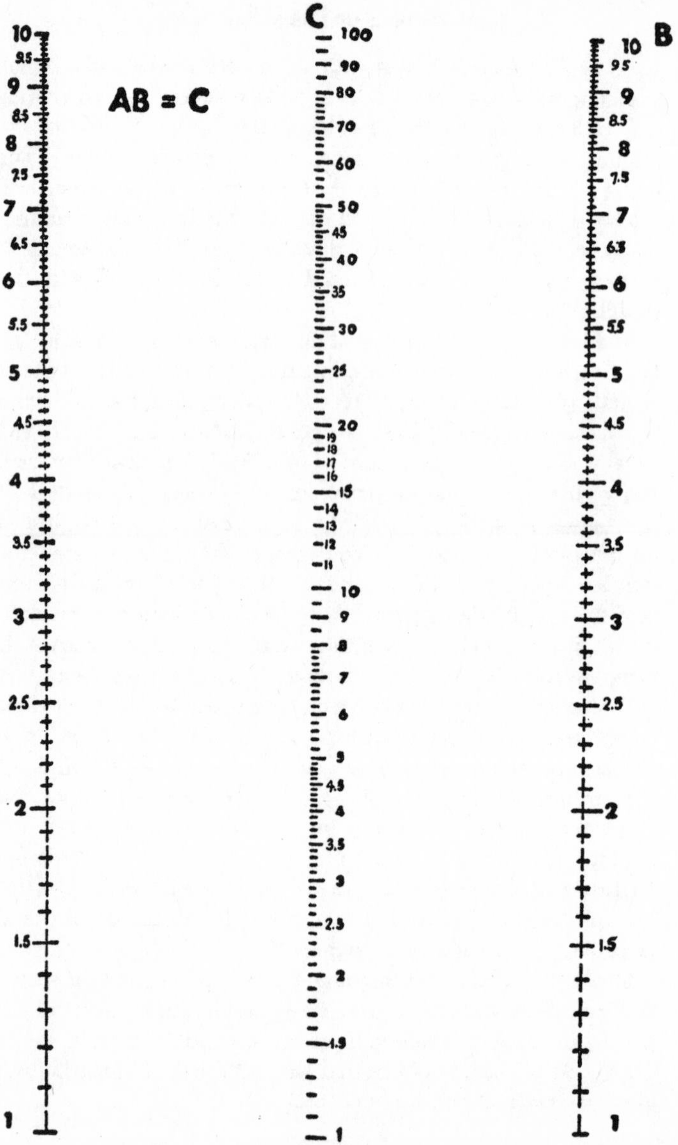

AB = C

FIGURE 45

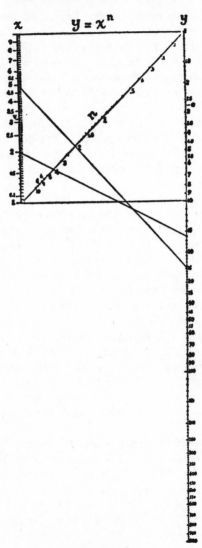

FIGURE 46

In Figure 46 we see two vertical lines x and y, each with a log or slide-rule scale. The x scale decreases from 10 to 1 and the y scale increases from 1 all the way to 1000. The nomograph is so constructed that the distance between the vertical lines is exactly equal to the x vertical scale from 10 to 1. Now notice the diagonal connecting the 1 on the x line with the 1 on the y line. This is, of course, the diagonal of a square so that the number 1 on this diagonal is exactly in the center of the square. This diagonal line is the power line which we shall call n. It is graduated in such a manner that any line connecting any number on x with any number on n and extended to meet y will instantly solve the power equation $y = x^n$.

In the diagram you will see a line drawn from 5 on x through 2 on n and meeting y at 25. This shows that $5^2 = 25$. If the same line from 5 were drawn through the 3 on n it would meet y halfway between the 100 and 150, so $5^3 = 125$. If you played around with your straightedge connecting any number on x with any number on n and extending the line, you will always get the value of y equal to x^n. A line from 3 on x through 2 on n meets y at 9: ($3^2 = 9$). A line from 3 on x through 4 on n meets y at 81 ($3^4 = 81$).

So you can get any number from 1 to 10 raised to any power all the way from .1 to 10 and if you extend the line x upward you will be able to get powers of numbers from 10 to 100 or 1000 or more, depending on how far upward you go. It is interesting to note that the farther up on the line x you travel, and the greater the power on line n which you connect with the numbers on the extended line, the more your straightedge will approach being parallel to the y line.

Notice now the fractional or decimal numbers to the right of the 1 on the diagonal line n. We know that $x^{.5}$ is the same as the square root of x and this can easily be checked by connecting 9 on x with .5 on n and noting that it cuts the 3 on y, showing that the square root of 9 is 3. In the same way you can show that the square root of 4 is 2. This remarkable nomograph will give you the answers to fractional powers or roots just as easily. Thus $3.5^{1.5}$

is 6.6, as you can verify by connecting 3.5 on x with 1.5 on n and extending it to y. In the same way you can get any other fractional or decimal power.

Of course this nomograph will give you roots merely by reversing the process. The cube root of 20, for example, is obtained by connecting 20 on y with 3 on n and extending it to meet x between 2.7 and 2.8. The fifth root of 5 is obtained by connecting the 5 on y with the 5 on n and extending it to meet x in 1.35.

A particularly interesting feature shows how 1 to any power is always 1. If you connect any of the numbers between 1 and 1.5 on x with any of the higher numbers (5, 6, 7 or 10) on n and extend the line, you will find that it cuts y in the lower number region: 1.1, for example, to the tenth power is approximately 2.7 (this approaches the Napierian base e). Obviously 1.01, which will be about 1/10 the distance between 1 and the first mark on x, would send the line up closer and closer to the 1 on the y line. When we get down to an inconceivably small fraction above 1 we reach the diagonal line itself.

You can make yourself a beautiful power nomograph similar to this one, only extended farther, by enlarging this nomograph and graduating the x, y and n lines even finer. All you need is an ordinary ruler. Here is the way to do it:

Lay off two slide-rule scales exactly alike and $6\frac{1}{4}''$ long as shown in the section on how to make a slide rule. Space these two scales exactly $6\frac{1}{4}''$ apart so that they form the vertical sides of a square as indicated in Figure 46. The X scale must have the 1 at the bottom and the Y scale the 1 at the top. Now extend the Y scale 3 times downward as shown, draw the diagonal from the 1 on the X scale to the 1 on the Y scale and you are all set. Connect 2 on X to 4 on Y and mark 2 where it crosses the diagonal. Check this point by connecting 3 on X to 9 on Y. The line should pass through this 2. Now connect 2 on X with 8 on Y and mark 3. Check by connecting 3 on X with 27 on Y. Keep doing this for other powers up to 5 or 6. Then join any number on X with the same number on Y and mark 1 on the diagonal. Now join 4 on X with 2 on Y and mark .5 on the diag-

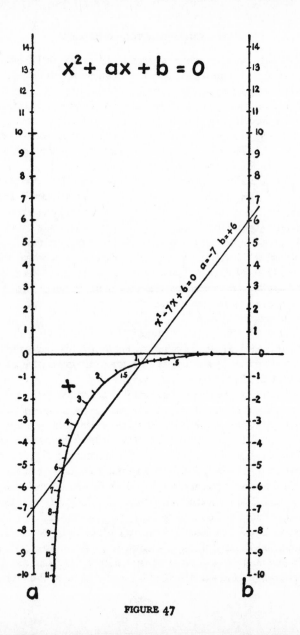

$$x^2 + ax + b = 0$$

$x^2 - 7x + 6 = 0 \quad a = -7 \quad b = +6$

FIGURE 47

onal. Check this by connecting 9 on X with 3 on Y. The line should pass through the same point. This is the square root point where $Y = \sqrt{X}$. Mark off the other points .1, .2, .3, .4, etc., and you now have a chart, made from an ordinary ruler, that will give you all the powers and roots of all numbers.

Of course the examples of nomographs shown here are about the simplest that can be made. They can be expanded as much as desired so that larger sums and products are obtained. If, for example, the A and B scales in Figure 45 were doubled and the C scale quadrupled, we would be multiplying two digit numbers, such as 24×38 and getting the result instantly on C.

Now let us look at Figure 47 which solves very simple quadratic equations instantly. Of course, every high-school student knows the famous formula for the solution of quadratic equations:

$$x = \frac{-b \pm \sqrt{b^2 - 4ac}}{2a}$$

but there is no need to do a lot of substitution work with a nomograph. Just use your ruler or straightedge! In the quadratic equation:

$$x^2 + ax + b = 0$$

a is represented by the left vertical line and b is represented by the right vertical line. All you need do to solve a simple quadratic equation is to connect a with b with your straightedge, just as you did before, and where it cuts the curved line x you can read the solution to the equation. The straight line in the diagram represents the solution of the quadratic equation $x^2 - 7x + 6 = 0$. Here $a = -7$ and $b = +6$. Connecting -7 on a with $+6$ on b, our line crosses 1 and 6 on the curved x line. 1 and 6 are therefore the correct roots of this equation, as you can easily verify by substitution. In a similar way the equation $x^2 - 2x + 1 = 0$ crosses the curved line at 1. Here a is -2 and b is $+1$. Connecting -2 on a to $+1$ on b, our straightedge passes through 1 on the curved x line.

Now try these simple examples yourself:

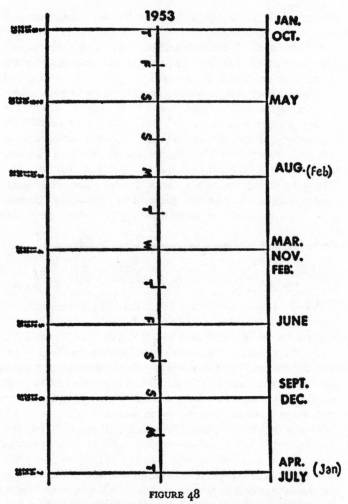

FIGURE 48

Note: For each successive year after 1953 merely move the center line one place to the left. January 1st, 1954 was on Friday (F), January 1st, 1955 on Saturday (S), etc. If you do this for each year you'll have a perpetual calendar.

$$x^2 - 7x + 12 = 0$$
$$x^2 - 3x + 2 = 0$$
$$x^2 - 5x + 6 = 0$$

Of course this is the simplest of all nomographs for quadratic equations. It gives only positive roots and is extremely limited. Nomographs involving parabolas and other curves have been worked out in great detail for solving all kinds of quadratic equations.

One of the most interesting of all nomographs, created and copyrighted by Harry D. Ruderman, is shown in Figure 48. By means of this diagram you can tell the day of the week any specific date will fall on. The center line, which is exactly equidistant from the lines at either side gives the days of the week in initials just as any calendar does. By means of each horizontal line read the months. The first one is either January or October. The second one is May. The third is either August or Leap Year February, etc. Note that the months in parenthesis have to do only with leap years. At the left of each horizontal line read the dates just as you do on a calendar. The first vertical line, for example, in intersecting a horizontal line represents any one of the numbers beside it. The same is true for all the horizontal lines where they intersect the vertical line. Now let us take a specific date in 1953. What day, for example, does September 21 fall on? Connecting the point where the horizontal line for September-December meets the vertical line with the point where the horizontal line showing 21 (the bottom one) meets the left line, our straightedge passes.through the letter M which is Monday. What day will the Fourth of July fall on in 1953? Connecting the July intersection with the horizontal containing 4 you will see at once that it will be Saturday, since it intersects the center line at S. Practice finding days on this chart and then consider the following: the diagram was made to fit the year 1953. It started off with Thursday because January 1 1953 is Thursday. If you want any day of any year, all you need do is change the day of January 1 on the middle line. In 1954, for example, the first-day reading on the middle line will be *F* (Friday) and all the other days will follow in regular order. The same is true for 1952. The middle day on the horizontal line corresponding to January 1 (leap year) will be *W* (Wednesday) and all the other days will follow in regular order. So here we have a simple nomograph, created by Harry D. Ruderman, which gives us a perpetual calendar.

MAKING A GOOD SLIDE RULE
WITH AN ORDINARY RULER

UNDOUBTEDLY you have seen or used a slide rule at some time or other and you know that it consists of a rule with a slide in it as shown in Figure 49. By moving the slide back and forth you can multiply and divide numbers very quickly, as well as do pro-

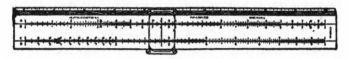

FIGURE 49

portion, take square and cube roots and raise to those powers. In one setting of the slide rule in each instance, you can get areas of circles from their diameters, transform inches to centimeters, quarts to liters, pounds to kilograms and do hundreds of other time-saving operations.

Slide rules are used in all engineering work and most branches of science. They are being used more and more in business today because they save hours of tedious work in multiplication and division, and also because they are light and small and will fit into the pocket. The better grades of slide rules sell anywhere from $5.00 to $25.00, but here is a way to make yourself an excellent slide rule with an ordinary ruler, the kind you buy at the ten-cent store. If you are careful you will be surprised how accurate your home-made slide rule will be, and you will be able to multiply, divide, take square and cube roots, do ratio and proportion, raise to powers and perform lots of other computations just by moving a strip of paper back and forth over another sheet of paper.

All you need for your homemade slide rule are two sheets of good drawing paper (bristol board is excellent), a very sharp, hard pencil (3H will do), a ruler and a little care. A magnifying glass will help, but it is not absolutely necessary if you take great care and are precise in making the first three marks on your slide rule. The entire accuracy of the rule will depend upon these first three marks, so it is essential that you do them with the utmost precision.

The first thing to do is to draw a line *exactly 6 1/4 inches long*. Mark each end of this line with very thin vertical lines and call each end 1. The left end is the "lower" 1 and the right end is the "upper" 1. Be sure that the distance between these two marks is *exactly* 6¼ inches—no more and no less. Now measure off *exactly* 1 7/8 inches from the lower 1, make another thin vertical mark, and call it 2. This is shown on Diagram *A*. Then measure *exactly* 2 31/32 inches from the lower 1; make a thin vertical line and call it 3. This, of course, is half of a sixteenth of an inch less than 3 inches, as shown in Diagram *A*. Finally make the same thin vertical mark at 5 9/32 inches and call it 7 as shown in *A*. You now have: 1, 2, 3, 7 and upper 1 on your sheet. If you have marked these off *with great care* your slide rule will be very useful; but if you have been careless you may be sure that you won't get reliable readings from it.

Now refer to Diagram *B*. It shows this scale, which we shall call *Y* for convenience. Directly below it place a movable strip of paper (which we shall call *X*) on the line and, *very carefully*, mark off the same lines on *X* so that the two papers, *X* and *Y*, are identical and the movable strip of paper, *X*, also has 1, 2, 3, 7 and upper 1 on it just exactly like the *Y* scale.

Now refer to Diagram *C*. It shows *X* moved to the right so that the lower 1 line on *X* is directly under the 2 line on *Y*. In this position mark off 4 on *Y* directly over the 2 on *X*, and 6 on *Y* directly over the 3 on *X*. It is very important that these markings be exact, as shown. You now have the *Y* scale with 1, 2, 3, 4, 6, 7 and upper

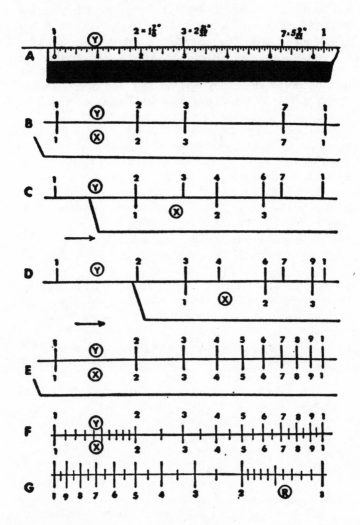

FIGURE 50

117

1. If you place the X scale so that lower 1 comes directly under the 4 on Y, you can mark off 8 on Y directly over the 2 on X. And by moving X so that the 1 comes directly under the 3 on Y, mark off 9 on Y directly over the 3 on X (Diagram D). Now you have all the numbers except 5 on the Y scale. To get the 5 just place the 2 on the X scale directly *under* the right-hand (the upper) 1 of Y and, directly over the lower 1 on the X scale mark off 5 on scale Y.

Now scale Y has all the numbers 1, 2, 3, 4, 5, 6, 7, 8, 9 and the right-hand 1. Place the movable strip or scale X in the same position it was in Diagram B and mark off the missing numbers on it. The scales should now be *absolutely identical* as shown in Diagram E.

At this point it is well to mark off 11 at exactly $\frac{1}{4}$ inch from the lower 1, and 13 at exactly 23/32 inch from that 1. Here is how to continue filling out the rest of the slide rule:

It is very important to note that although the 2, 3, 4, 5, 6, 7, 8 and 9 are unit digits, they are also 20, 30, 40, 50, 60, 70, 80 and 90 or 200, 300, 400, 500, etc.

In the same way the 25, 35, 45, etc., are $2\frac{1}{2}$, $3\frac{1}{2}$, $4\frac{1}{2}$, $5\frac{1}{2}$, etc., or 250, 350, 450, 550, etc. All multiples of 10 are in the same place on the slide rule so the decimal place makes no difference.

Place the 2 of X under the 3 of Y and mark off 1.5 or 15 above the left-hand 1 on X. Also mark off 4.5 or 45 on Y directly over the 3 on X.

Place the 2 of X under the 5 of Y and mark off 2.5 or 25 above the left-hand 1 on X.

Place the 2 of X under the 7 of Y and mark off 3.5 or 35 above the left-hand 1 on X.

Place the 2 of X under the 9 of Y and mark off 4.5 or 45 above the left-hand 1 on X.

Divide the spaces between 8 and 9 and 9 and upper 1 in half for 8.5 and 9.5.

Place the left-hand 1 of X under the 11 on Y and mark off

5.5 or 55 on Y above the 5 on X. Do the same for the 13 on Y and mark off 6.5 or 65 on Y.

Now place the left-hand 1 on X under the 15 on Y and mark off 7.5 or 75 on Y directly over the 5 on X.

Now place the 5 on X under the 6 on Y and mark off 1.2 or 12 on Y above the left-hand 1 on X. Do the same for the 7 on Y and mark off 1.4 or 14 on Y above the left-hand 1 on X.

Your upper scale now has 11, 12, 13, 14, 15 marked off in it as well as 20, 25, 30, 35, 40, 45, 50, 55, 60, 65, 70, 75, 80, 85, 90, 95 and the right-hand 1, as shown in Diagram F.

From now on it is easy. Place the left-hand 1 successively under 11, 12, 13 and use the 2 mark on the X scale to mark off 22, 24, 26, and 28 between the 2 and 3 on Y. To get 16, 17, 18 and 19 on Y place the 5 on X under the 95, 90, 85 and 80 of Y respectively, and mark off 19, 18, 17 and 16 above the left-hand 1 on X.

Now, as before, you can get 32, 34, 36, and 38 the way you got 22, 24, 26, and 28. Smaller divisions may be done by the eye.

By now the Y scale is fairly complete and it won't take much more work to complete it entirely. This done, mark off all the same spacing on the X scale so that you have two identical scales as shown in Diagram H, Figure 51. Now you are ready to use the homemade slide rule.

If you want to expand your work and add more features to your slide rule, all you need do is make an exact duplicate of the X or Y scale, turn it upside down and number it as before. Place this new scale, which we shall call the R scale, directly under the X scale as shown in Diagram G and you have all the decimal equivalents by direct reading. You can see at once that if all the numbers are fractions and the 2, 3, 4, 5, etc., become $\frac{1}{2}$, $\frac{1}{3}$, $\frac{1}{4}$, $\frac{1}{5}$ and so on, then $\frac{1}{2}$ on the X scale comes directly over .5 on the R scale and $\frac{1}{4}$ on the X scale comes to .25 on the R scale. In the same way you can read off all the fractions as decimal equivalents: thus from Diagram G we get ½ is .5, 1/3 is .333, ¼ is .25, 1/5 is .2, 1/6 is .166, 1/7 is .4, 1/8 is .125 and 1/9 is .11, etc.

This R scale is the reciprocal scale and it is nothing more than the regular scale reversed. You can multiply numbers by means of this scale by doing just the reverse of what you do with the X scale. To multiply 3 by 15 with X and Y scales you put the 1 of the X scale under the 3 of the Y scale and look above 15 on the X scale to find 45 on the Y scale. It's just the other way with the R scale. Here you put the 3 of the R scale over the 15 of the X scale and look under the right-hand 1 of the R scale. You will find 45 on the Y scale.

If you are ambitious enough to make another scale from the X or Y scale, and make it just twice as large, or 12½ inches long, by laying off exactly twice the distances on the 12½-inch line that you did on the 6¼-inch line, and then place two X scales directly above the new scale, you will see that everything on the two X scales (side by side) will be the *square* of everything on the new scale.

The slide rule that you have now made is the "mathematical equivalent" of commercial slide rules costing one dollar or more. Of course the commercial slide rules are more accurate than yours because they are made by machine, and are more convenient because they are made of wood, plastic or metal. In addition, a commercial slide rule will have scales for squaring, for cubing and extracting square and cube roots, as well as sines, cosines, tangents, logarithms and many other functions. The Y scale on your slide rule is usually called the D scale. The X scale is called the C scale, and the R the *CI* or *C-Inverted* scale.

HOW TO USE YOUR SLIDE RULE

To MULTIPLY on the slide rule you must use either of the two 1's on the X scale and apply them under the number you want to multiply on the Y scale. You must also remember that everything on the slide rule scale is a power of 10 and it is up to you to supply the proper decimal place. You know very well that 16 × 20, for example, is not 32 but 320. It will be at 3.2 on the scale so it is up to you to give it the proper decimal place. 51 × 60 will show up as 3.06 on the scale. You know very well that it is in the thousands so it must be 3060. If you remember the decimal part of the slide rule you will have no trouble at all. One more thing: This homemade slide rule, no matter how carefully you have made it, will not be accurate to four or even three decimal places. To multiply 17 by 38, for example, you know that it must end in 6 since 7 × 8 is 56. It is up to you to supply the last digit—the slide rule will supply the first two.

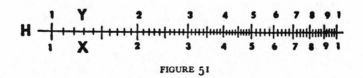

FIGURE 51

Now that you have made your slide rule so that it resembles Figure 51 (the five marks can be eliminated after 5 and the submarks are in two's) multiply 14 by 27. Move the 1 on the X scale directly under the 14 (the fourth division after the 1 which is 1.4) on the Y scale and, directly above the 27 (2.7) on the Y scale read 3.7 "nearly 3.8." Now you know that the result ends in 8 so the answer must be 378 which it is. Try another example. Multiply 53 by 23. Move the upper right 1 on the X scale directly under the 53 on the Y scale and, directly over the 23 on the X scale read 1.2 "and a little bit over." Now you know that 20 × 50 is 1000 so the result must be about 1200. We know that it ends in 9 since 3 × 3 = 9 and it is about 1/5 the way between 1.2 and 1.3. It must, therefore, be 1219. Now try these: 13 × 41; 22 × 17; 16 × 41; 31 × 15; 19 × 38.

Of course division is just the opposite. To divide 48 by 4, just place the 4 on the X scale directly under the 4.8 on the Y scale and refer back to the left 1 on X. Directly above it read 1.2 which, of course, is 12 in this case. Divide 65 by 22: Move the 2.2 on the X scale directly under the 6.5 (half way between the 6 and 7) on the Y scale and, over the left-hand 1 on the X scale, read 2.95. Divide 13 by 2: move the 1.3 on the X scale under the 2 on the Y scale and, over the right-hand 1 on X, read 6.5. Now try the following for practice: $64 \div 32$; $87 \div 3$; $14 \div 7$; $734 \div 12$.

Proportions are easy on the slide rule. Try the following: $3 : 5 = 7 : ?$ Move the 3 on X under the 5 on Y, and over the 6 on X read upper 1 (10) on Y. Now move this 6 on X under the left-hand 1 on Y and, over 7 on X, read 11.75. Study this a while and you will see that once you have the X scale set against the Y scale at any ratio, all the numbers on both these scales will be the same ratio. Set 2 under 3 and see 4 under 6 and 6 under 9, etc.

BIRD'S-EYE VIEW OF PLANE

TRIGONOMETRY

THIS ORIGINAL chart (Figure 53) makes trigonometry child's play. By using it you can get all the sides and angles of a right triangle almost instantly and you don't need to look up the sine or cosine or tangent in the tables, either.

The curved lines represent the hypotenuses and bases of the right triangle, while the horizontal lines measure the height of the vertical side. The protractor gives you the angle instantly and that is all you need. Here are a few problems:

In right triangle *ABC*, angle *A* is 47° 30′ and the hypotenuse is 15 inches. What are the lengths of *a* and *b*? All you need do is put a straightedge (or draw a light line) from *O* through the 47° 30′ mark on the protractor and look where it crosses the curved line 15. If you do this you will see that it meets it at 11 which is the side *a*. Now draw a perpendicular to the base from this point and get 10.1 for *b*.

Here is another: given side *a* = 12 and *c* = 22, find the angles and the other side. All you need do is find curved line 22, and follow it around till it meets horizontal line 12. Connect this with *O* and extend it through the protractor to get the angle of 33° 15′. Drop a perpendicular to the base and get 18.5. That's all there is to it.

Suppose we have side *a* = 17 and side *b* = 8.5. What is the angle *A*? Find 8.5 at the base of the chart and run a perpendicular up to the 17th horizontal line. Connect this point with *O* and

TABLE

Angle	Sin	Cos	
0°	0.000	1.000	90°
1	0.017	1.000	89
2	0.035	0.999	88
3	0.052	0.999	87
4	0.070	0.998	86
5°	0.087	0.996	85°
6	0.105	0.995	84
7	0.122	0.993	83
8	0.139	0.990	82
9	0.156	0.988	81
10°	0.174	0.985	80°
11	0.191	0.982	79
12	0.208	0.978	78
13	0.225	0.974	77
14	0.242	0.970	76
15°	0.259	0.966	75°
16	0.276	0.961	74
17	0.292	0.956	73
18	0.309	0.951	72
19	0.326	0.946	71
20°	0.342	0.940	70°
21	0.358	0.934	69
22	0.375	0.927	68
23	0.391	0.921	67
24	0.407	0.914	66
25°	0.423	0.906	65°
26	0.438	0.899	64
27	0.454	0.891	63
28	0.469	0.883	62
29	0.485	0.875	61
30°	0.500	0.866	60°
31	0.515	0.857	59
32	0.530	0.848	58
33	0.545	0.839	57
34	0.559	0.829	56
35°	0.574	0.819	55°
36	0.588	0.809	54
37	0.602	0.799	53
38	0.616	0.788	52
39	0.629	0.777	51
40°	0.643	0.766	50°
41	0.656	0.755	49
42	0.669	0.743	48
43	0.682	0.731	47
44	0.695	0.719	46
45°	0.707	0.707	45°
	Cos	Sin	Angle

FIGURE 52

124

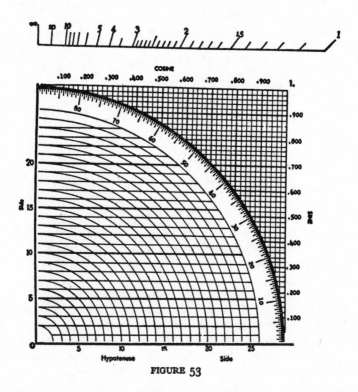

FIGURE 53

extend it through the protractor to read the angle of 64°. The hypotenuse, incidentally, from this chart is 18.9.

All these values are remarkably accurate and the more you play around with this chart the more fun you'll have with plane trigonometry. The values of the natural sines and cosines are given in the upper part. Each line represents 2. Compare these values with those given in Figure 52 and you will see how close they come. Take the sine of 66° for example. Look at the horizontal line from 65°, and see that it is .900, and 66° is .91, which compares with .914 in the table. Take any other sine or cosine and check it with

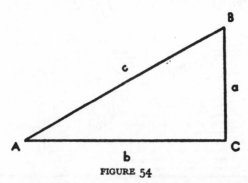

FIGURE 54

the table, and you will be surprised how closely they agree. Of course you can solve any problem with regard to the right triangle almost instantly and with no thought at all by means of this remarkable chart.

Tangents may also be found by extending the line from O to the vertical edge of the sines or by extending it (for angles greater than 45°) to the horizontal line directly above the cosines.

In addition to solving the right triangle completely in a small fraction of the time it takes to solve it by the regulation means of looking up the logs and log sines or log cosines, this chart verifies many of the trigonometric formulas and identities quickly and clearly.

Take, for example, the familiar:

$$SIN^2 A + COS^2 A = 1$$

Take A at 53° and we have from the chart: $\sin A = .8$, $\cos A = .6$

$$.8^2 + .6^2 = 1.00$$

The same is true for the complement of the angle or 37°: $\sin A = .6$ and $\cos A = .8$ and the sum of their squares is again 1.

This can be done again and again on the chart for angles and their complements: sin 60° = .5 from the chart; cos 60° = .86 ($\frac{1}{2}\sqrt{3}$), and we have $.86^2 + .5^2 = 1.00$.

The chart gives an instant test of many of the well-known trigonometric formulas, for example:

$$\text{SIN} (X + Y) = \text{SIN } X \text{ COS } Y + \text{COS } X \text{ SIN } Y$$

Suppose x is 32° and y is 28°; then $x + y = 60°$.

> From the chart: sin 32° = .53; cos 32° = .85 (sin and cos x)
> sin 28° = .47; cos 28° = .88 (sin and cos y)
> Then sin x cos y = .53 × .88 = .467
> and cos x sin y = .85 × .47 = .399
> .866 which is sin 60°.

Now test one yourself. Take $x = 17°$ and $y = 36°$, and show from the chart that sin 53° = sin 17° cos 36° + cos 17° sin 36°.

Take another familiar formula:

$$\text{SIN } 2 X = 2 \text{ SIN } X \text{ COS } X$$

> Take $x = 18°$ then sin 18° = .31 from the chart
> cos 18° = .95 from the chart
> Then 2 sin x cos x = 2(.31 × .95) = 2 × .2945 = .5890

Now draw the angle 36° on the chart (twice 18°) and see that sin 36° is .589.

Try this one for yourself. Take $x = 35°$, and see that sin 70° is equal to 2 (sin 35° cos 35°) directly from the chart.

Here is another familiar formula:

$$\text{SIN} (X - Y) = \text{SIN } X \text{ COS } Y - \text{COS } X \text{ SIN } Y$$

Take $x = 47°$ and $y = 13°$, and run it through the same as you did with the sin $(x + y)$, showing that sin 34° (47 − 13) equals sin x cos y − cos x sin y, which in turn is .558.

In a similar manner you can check from the chart that

$$\text{COS } 2X = \text{COS}^2 X - \text{SIN}^2 X$$

and, in fact, you can instantly see the truth of most trigonometric formulas and identities, without the use of tables and elaborate multiplication or logarithmic additions. By making a copy of this chart and enlarging it greatly so that your lines will take in a much greater scope, you can solve problems in plane trigonometry very quickly and painlessly, and have a lot of fun doing them.

From the chart solve the following right triangles completely, given:

1. Angle $A = 48°$; $a = 13$
2. $b = 7$; $a = 12$
3. Hypotenuse $= 15$; angle $B = 42°$
4. Hypotenuse $= 10$, $a = 6$
5. Hypotenuse $= 25$; $b = 22$.

Prove the following by means of the chart:

1. $\text{TAN } X = \dfrac{\text{SIN } X}{\text{COS } X}$
2. $\text{SIN}^2 X - \text{SIN}^2 Y = \text{SIN } (X + Y) \times \text{SIN } (X - Y)$
3. $\text{SIN } \frac{1}{2}X = \sqrt{\frac{1}{2} (1 - \text{COS } X)}$
4. $\text{COS } \frac{1}{2}X = \sqrt{\frac{1}{2} (1 + \text{COS } X)}$

CURVES THAT CONTROL
OUR LIVES

CERTAIN mathematical curves are extremely important to us. Among these are the circle, the ellipse, the parabola and the hyperbola. All are sections of a right circular cone and so they are called *conic sections*. The circle and the ellipse are the most familiar, but the other two are very important too, even though we are not so well acquainted with them. Now look at Figure 55. In *A*, a plane cuts the cone parallel to the base and the resulting section is a circle. In *B* a plane cuts the cone on a slant and the resulting section is an ellipse. In *C* a plane cuts the cone parallel to the slant

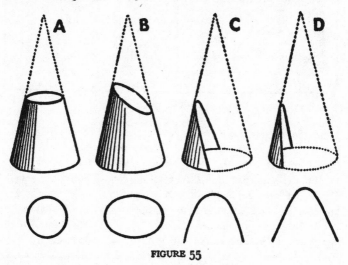

FIGURE 55

height, and the resulting section is a parabola. In *D* the plane cuts the cone perpendicular to the base and the resulting section is a hyperbola.

You can easily prove this to yourself and you don't need anything more than an ordinary flashlight and one of the walls of your room. The light comes out of a flashlight in the form of a cone. Your wall is a plane; so all you need do is to focus the beam of light on the wall, holding the flashlight at different angles. In

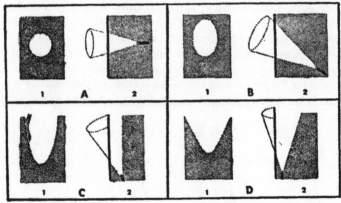

FIGURE 56

Figure 56 we see how this is done. Each section of this figure has two parts. The right-hand part (2) shows the position of the flashlight with respect to the wall (shown in section by a black line) and the left-hand part shows the resulting spot of light on the wall (1). In *A* we see the flashlight held at right angles to the wall (2), and the wall is therefore a plane cutting the beam parallel to its base. The result is a circle of light (1). In *B* we see the beam of light thrown slantingly at the wall and the wall is therefore a plane cutting the beam slantingly (2). The result is an ellipse of light on the wall (1). In *C* the beam has one side parallel to the wall so the wall cuts it parallel to the slant height of the cone that the beam forms and the result is a parabola of light on the wall (1). In *D* we see the beam's center parallel to the wall (2) and the result is a hyperbola (1).

THE CIRCLE

THIS IS BY far the most important thing ever invented by man. Nowhere does a perfect circle occur in nature. So man can take a bow and full credit for discovering it. Just try to imagine a civilization if there were no such curve as the circle. Transportation over land would be on horseback and muleback, or the backs of other animals. Machinery of any and every type from the simplest to the most complex would be impossible. Life would certainly be primitive without machinery or vehicles and we would all be living like the savages. The wheel, whether it be used for transportation or in machinery is the greatest of all inventions in the entire history of man. Thank the circle for everything that you have today.

It is interesting to investigate what is really meant by a circle. Strictly speaking, and from a purely mathematical point of view, the circle is the area bounded by a circumference. Take away the circumference and the circle vanishes. The circumference, then, is not the circle but the boundary of a closed area called a circle. By common usage, however, the line itself is called a circle. It is defined as the locus of a point whose path is always at the same distance from a point within, called the center. The radius, of course, is the distance from the center to the circumference and is denoted by the letter r. So the circle has only one center and a constant radius and that is why all circles are the "same shape." One circle is larger or smaller than another only because its radius is longer or shorter and for no other reason. The area of a circle is πr^2 and the length of its circumference is $2\pi r$. In the section called *More and More of Less and Less* we saw how these vitally important formulas are derived.

Imagine a man who has had one drink too many looking at a circle. He would probably see it elongated with two centers instead of one and a short radius and a long radius. A queer circle indeed, but in reality nothing more than

THE ELLIPSE

THE ELLIPSE has no radius and no center as such. Four elliptical wheels on an automobile with the axle through their geometric center would not make for comfortable riding, as you can well imagine. The ellipse has a major axis and a minor axis and two points called *foci*. Of course, you can see that in this case there can be thousands of differently shaped ellipses merely by varying the

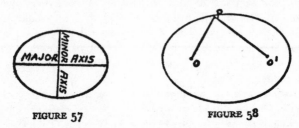

FIGURE 57   FIGURE 58

lengths of the two axes (Figure 57). The semimajor and the semi-minor axes (the half axes) are denoted by the letters a and b respectively and the area is πab. The circumference of an ellipse is not so easily calculated and requires an advanced mathematical process known as rectification. When $a = b$, the ellipse becomes a circle of radius a or b, and the greater the ratio of the lengths of a and b, the more elongated will be the ellipse. The ellipse is important to all of us since the earth's orbit around the sun is not a circle but an ellipse, and so are the orbits of all the other planets.

In perspective drawing and certain forms of art the ellipse plays an important part, since all circles, tops of cylinders, etc., when viewed slanting from above or below the eye level, turn out to be ellipses. One interesting feature of an ellipse is that the sum of the

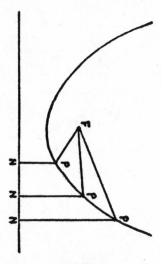

FIGURE 59

two lines joining the two foci with the ellipse is always the same. In Figure 58, $PO + O'P$ always equals the same number. Another interesting feature is the fact that a beam of light sent out from one focus O and striking the elliptical ceiling anywhere between O and O' will be reflected back through O'. The same is true for sound waves and hence the famous whispering gallery in the Capitol in Washington, D. C. If you stand at one point and whisper ever so faintly, you can be heard at another point fifty or one hundred feet away. These two points are foci of a large ellipse and the faint sound is reflected from one focus to the other only, and to no other point.

THE PARABOLA

IF YOU could "pull an ellipse out" the way you do taffy, and stretch the distance between O and O' more and more, you would find that the ellipse would approach the shape of a parabola and,

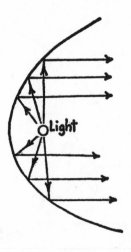

FIGURE 60

indeed, when one focus becomes infinitely far from the other the ellipse becomes the parabola. A parabola may be defined as the locus of a point that moves so that its distance from a given point is always equal to its distance from a given straight line. In Figure 59 we have the point P whose distance from the focus F of the parabola to the line is always the same or, in other words, $PF = PN$, and the path of the point P is always the apex of an isosceles triangle. Of course, the parabola is not a closed curve and therefore has no area since it goes off to infinity on both sides of the focus F. The parabola is the curve taken by a projectile or bullet, assuming a minimum of air resistance, and consequently a thorough knowledge of it is essential to those in the artillery and to students of ballistics. Acoustic engineers must have a good knowledge of the parabola and its equivalent solid, the paraboloid. And that important curve is useful to us at night when we are driving because all automobile and locomotive headlight reflectors are paraboloids. Each ray of light that leaves the focus F and strikes the surface of the paraboloid is reflected parallel to the axis of the parabola as shown in Figure 60. The headlight then throws a straight beam without any fixed focus, which is a great advantage to the driver at night. The great Palomar telescope would not be possible without the parabola. The famous 200-inch mirror is not a section of a sphere but a section of a parabola—actually a section of a paraboloid. All rays coming from far out in space strike this mirror and are brought to a focus: just the reverse of the automobile headlight.

THE HYPERBOLA

LITTLE CAN be said of the last curve from the practical point of view. But the curve is extremely important in higher mathematics, and an entire branch of trigonometry is based on it. Just as the sine, cosine, tangent, etc., are circular functions and come from parts of a circle, measured in degrees, so these other functions, known as hyperbolic functions, are parts of a hyperbola and called sinh, cosh, tanh, etc., the h standing for hyperbola. One of the curves in nature is the hyperbolic cosine, otherwise known as the catenary. It is the curve of a loose chain supported at both ends, and looks much like a parabola. This is an extremely important curve in suspension-bridge design.

So you can see that these conic sections are useful and important to us. The ellipse, the parabola and the hyperbola all occur in nature. The orbits of the planets are ellipses and the path of a baseball thrown from the outfield to home plate is a parabola, as is the path of any object thrown slantingly into the air. The hyperbola is sometimes the path of comets but it very seldom occurs otherwise in nature. It is important chiefly from a mathematical standpoint and, the most important of all, the circle, unknown in Nature, is the crowning achievement of man.

MATHEMATICAL HOW-TO-DO'S

1. Here is a simple way to find the center of a circle without bothering to erect perpendiculars on the sides of an inscribed triangle. First get the diameter by applying the edge of a sheet of paper or a card to the circumference as shown in Figure 61. If you now mark where the sides of the sheet meet the circumference

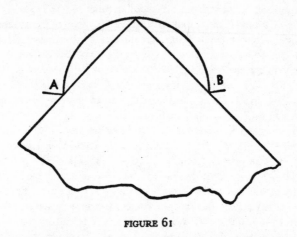

FIGURE 61

(at *A* and *B*) you will have the diameter *AB*. This is because all commercial paper is cut at right angles, so any corner is 90°. Since a right angle always subtends an arc of 180°, which is a semicircle, the line *AB* must be the diameter. But the center of the circle is the mid-point of this diameter so all we need do is draw another diameter by the same method and where the two intersect will be the center of the circle.

2. To tell how far the horizon is from where you are use this formula:

$$D \text{ (in miles)} = \sqrt{\frac{8 \text{ (distance above ground in feet)}}{5}}$$

If you are standing on the beach and are six feet tall the horizon will be $\sqrt{48/5}$ or 3.1 miles away. If you are in an airplane flying two miles above the sea level the horizon will be

$$D = \sqrt{\frac{8 \times 10560}{5}} \quad \text{or} \quad \sqrt{16896} \text{ which is 130 miles away.}$$

3. To divide a line into any number of equal parts simply draw another line of suitable length at any angle to the given line and measure off the required number of equal divisions on this line as

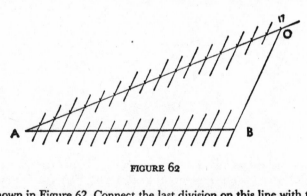

FIGURE 62

shown in Figure 62. Connect the last division on this line with the end of the given line and draw parallel lines to this connecting line through each division. These parallel lines will divide the given line into the required number of parts. The line *AB* in Figure 62 is $2^7/_8''$ long, and must be divided into 17 equal parts. The line *AO* is drawn at any angle and at such length that it can be divided into 17 equal parts by a ruler. The 17th part is then connected with the point B and parallel lines are drawn through the other divisions on AO. They divide AB into 17 equal parts.

4. To divide a circle into any number of equal parts (up to twenty), draw the diameter and divide it into the required number of parts by the method just explained. Now, from each end of the

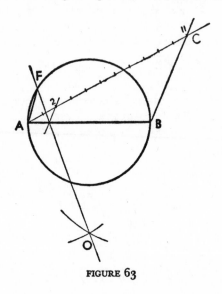

FIGURE 63

diameter and with it as a radius, swing two arcs below the circle meeting at a point O, as shown in Figure 63. Through O draw a line passing through the *second* division on your diameter and cutting the circumference at F. The arc AF is the required arc. In this case it is one eleventh of the circumference.

It must be mentioned that this is not an exact division; but it is so nearly exact that there is practically no difference. For all divisions less than twenty this method is very practical, even though it is not entirely accurate from a purely geometrical standpoint.

5. To lay off a right angle on the ground. In laying out a tennis court or a baseball diamond or any other large area where right angles are necessary, just measure with a steel tape 6 feet in one direction and 8 feet at *approximately* 90° to it. Now swing a short arc in the earth with this 8 foot length and measure 10 feet from the end of the 6 foot line to this arc. This will give you a 6 = 8 = 10 triangle, which is a right triangle with the right angle where you want it. Figure 64 shows you the principle.

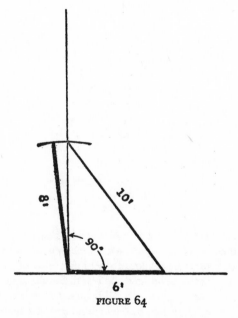

FIGURE 64

6. To count seconds without a watch or clock. In timing a race seconds are very important. Suppose you want to time a runner

and you have no timepiece of any description. How do you measure seconds?

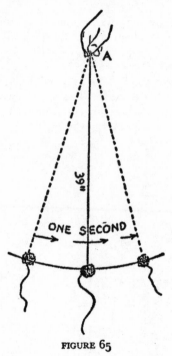

FIGURE 65

First find a piece of string at least five feet long. Now measure off from one end of the string (which we shall call A) a length just *three times* the distance from your elbow to the center of your palm. Knot the string at this point, and the length from that knot to the beginning of the string (point A) will be about 39 inches. Now tie a stone or some other weight to the knotted end, disregarding the rest of the string as shown in Figure 65. Now hold the string at A and let it swing like a pendulum, for that is just what it is. The time it takes to make one swing in one direction will be one second.

7. To find the distance objects are from you by means of triangles. In this case you must know the height of the object. Suppose you are sitting on your porch and there is a farmhouse on a mountain opposite. To get the approximate distance of that farmhouse you have to decide its height first. You must know that most farmhouses have two stories and an attic and come to about 25 or 30 feet. That is close enough. Now all you need to do is take a foot rule and, holding it one foot from your eye, measure what part of an inch the distant farmhouse comes to on the ruler. Suppose it measures $\frac{1}{4}''$, then we have the proportion

$$12 : \frac{1}{4} = x : 25 \times 12''$$
$$\text{or} \quad 12 : \frac{1}{4} = x : 300''$$
$$\text{then} \quad \frac{1}{4}x = 3600''$$
$$\text{hence} \quad x = 4 \times 3600'' = 14400''$$
$$\text{or} \quad x = 1200 \text{ feet}$$

You can understand that everything was reduced to inches in the above example because the farmhouse seemed to be only $\frac{1}{4}''$ high when you held the ruler 12 inches from your eye. It is best to figure everything in inches and then reduce the result to feet. Obviously if that same farmhouse appeared to be only 1/16 of an inch high on the ruler, it would be four times as far away or nearly a mile.

The same rule may be reversed and you can find how high an object is if you know its distance from you. If a smokestack 200 feet from you measures $1\frac{1}{2}$ inches on your ruler when you hold it one foot from your eyes, you can figure as follows:

$$12 : 1\frac{1}{2} = (200 \times 12) : x$$
$$12 : 1\frac{1}{2} = 2400 : x$$
$$12x = 3600$$
$$x = 300'' \text{ or } 25'$$

8. To determine how large or small a picture will become and see it on paper before sending it to the photographers, photostaters or photoengravers, place a sheet of tracing paper over it and enclose the entire picture in a rectangle. Suppose the picture measures 3 15/16'' by 2 $\frac{1}{4}$'' and you want to reduce it so that it is 1 inch

high. To find the other dimension draw the diagonal of the rectangle which you drew on the tracing paper and which enclosed the picture, and measure off 1 inch on the shorter side. At this

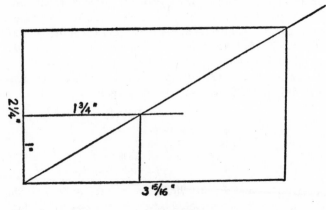

FIGURE 66

point draw a line at right angles to the side. The length of this line from the side of the rectangle to the diagonal will be the length of the other side of the reduced picture. This is shown in Figure 66 and if you measure it you will see it is 1¾″ long. So the reduced picture will be 1″ × 1¾″.

To see how this reduced picture will look on a sheet of paper, cut out a rectangle that is 1″ × 1¾″ and hold it at such a distance in front of the picture that the picture completely fills the opening. This will show you the picture reduced to the size you want on a sheet of paper just the way it will appear when printed.

9. Here is a simple and practical way to make accurate reproductions of your favorite pictures. Suppose you have the small picture of a ball player and you want to draw it just twice its size. Divide the picture into a number of squares by drawing vertical and horizontal lines at equal distances apart as shown in Figure

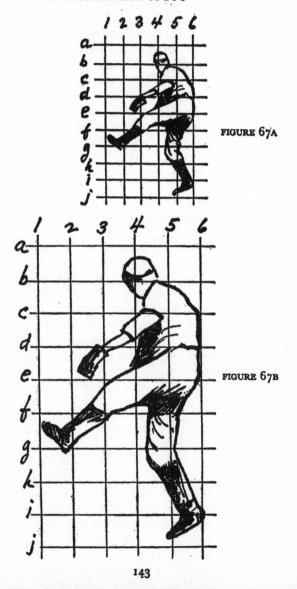

FIGURE 67A

FIGURE 67B

143

67A. Now number the vertical lines *1, 2, 3, 4,* etc., and letter the horizontal lines *a, b, c, d,* etc. The next thing to do is draw similar lines just twice as far apart on another sheet of paper, numbering and lettering them just as you did before. The new squares will then be four times the area of the original squares, Figure *67B*. Now start to draw in the picture with reference to the numbered and lettered lines. If you examine Figure *67B* you will see that the pitcher's left foot starts near *f–1* and the heel is near *g–2,* then the sock extends from *g–2* to *f–3* and the leg goes all the way over to *e–6.* The pitcher's back extends along the *6* line from *e* to *c* and then slants over to *b–5.* You can go on from there and you will be amazed how easily and accurately your enlargement develops. Of course the guidelines should be done very lightly in pencil so they can be erased after the picture is inked in.

10. To draw an ellipse with a compass, draw a rhombus *ACBD* (Figure 68) and bisect the angles by the two lines *AB* and *DC.* For the best result the angles *A, C, B,* and *D* should be 60° each so you have two equilateral triangles with a common vertical side *CD.* Now draw *CF* and *CH* bisecting the angles at *C* and meeting the sides *AD* and *DB* at 90°. Do the same with *DE* and *DG.* These lines intersect at *O* and *O'.* With these points as centers and *OE* as a radius draw arc *FE.* Do the same with arc *GH.* With *D* as a center and a radius equal to *DE* draw arc *EG* and with *C* as a center and a radius equal to *CF* draw arc *FH.* These two arcs will meet the arcs *FE* and *GH* and an excellent ellipse will be formed as shown in Figure 68. Of course all construction lines must be done lightly in pencil so they may be easily erased after the ellipse is inked in.

11. In case you should forget the various formulas for the volumes of regular solids like the sphere, the cone of revolution, the frustum of a cone, the cylinder and many others, here is *one* formula that can be applied to all of these solids and many more. It is one

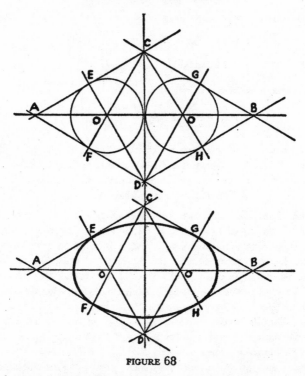

FIGURE 68

of the most remarkable formulas in mathematics and is known as the prismoidal formula. Here it is:

$$\frac{B + 4M + T}{6} \times h$$

where B is the area of the bottom, M the area of the middle, T the area of the top and h the height of the solid. Now let us apply this to some of the solids we mentioned above. Take the sphere:

$$B = 0 \qquad M = \pi r^2 \qquad T = 0 \qquad h = 2r$$

$$\frac{0 + 4\pi r^2 + 0}{6} \times 2r = \frac{8\pi r^3}{6} = \frac{4}{3}\pi r^3$$

Now take a cone of revolution:

$$B = \pi r^2 \qquad M = \frac{\pi r^2}{4} \qquad T = 0 \qquad h = h$$

$$\frac{\pi r^2 + \pi r^2 + 0}{6} \times h = \frac{1}{3} \pi r^2 h$$

Now take a cylinder:

$$B = \pi r^2 \qquad M = \pi r^2 \qquad T = \pi r^2 \qquad h = h$$

$$\frac{\pi r^2 + 4\pi r^2 + \pi r^2}{6} \times h = \pi r^2 h$$

This remarkable formula works for almost any other regular solid like a pyramid, a cube and a frustum of a cone. Try it and see. It is an extremely simple formula to memorize and acts as a sort of skeleton key for these volumes of solids.

12. The table on page 148 enables you to tell how high your house is, or how high any tall tree or flagpole or building is, anywhere in the United States. It is based on a very simple formula which navigators use in "shooting the sun." This formula tells us the angle of the sun above the horizon at noon, and is: *90° minus your latitude + the sun's declination above or below the celestial equator* (the imaginary projection of the earth's equator and the sky). This declination varies from +23½° on June 21 to −23½° on December 21 and on March 21 and September 21 it is zero. (These dates are approximate.) Starting on March 21 the sun crosses the celestial equator and starts getting higher and higher in the sky at noon. The celestial equator is always *90° minus the latitude,* so that the higher the sun gets above the celestial equator, the greater the angle that must be added to this value. On June 21, the first day of summer, the sun is at a maximum, 23½° above the celestial equator. After June 21 the sun starts to get lower every day, crossing the celestial equator again on September 21 and going as far as 23½° below it by the first day of winter, December 21. This it keeps doing year after year, century after century. So the length of shadows at noon vary every day with the date, and also with the latitude, and consequently the angle *x* in the diagram also varies with the date and the latitude.

The table has been carefully worked out for every two degrees of latitude and for each ten-day period of each month. What you see in these numbers is the tangent of the angle the noon sun makes with the horizontal shadow; if this is multiplied by the length of this horizontal shadow at noon you will have the height of the house or tall pine tree or flagpole or building in question. Let us take a few examples:

Suppose you live in a suburb of Chicago and on August 14 you want to know how high that flagpole is in front of your house. Just measure its shadow at noon, look at the map in Figure 69 for the latitude of Chicago (42°), and then on the chart for the date (between 10–20 August). Now multiply the length of the shadow by the number you find. The date is August 14, and suppose the

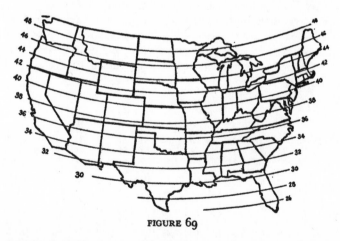

FIGURE 69

length of the shadow at noon is 16 feet. Chicago is about 42° latitude so, in the 42° column, look for the nearest date to August 14. You will find it in August 10–20 and the number is 1.8. The pole in front of your house is therefore 1.8 × 16 feet high or 28.8 feet high. The same pole will cast a shadow at noon on December 21 of 28.8 feet divided by .47, or 61.3 feet.

In a similar way you can tell how long your shadow will be at any place and at any time just by dividing instead of multiplying. Suppose you are 5.5 feet tall, how long will your shadow be on the following dates and in the following places?

> Seattle, Washington, on April 21? (46° latitude)
> Miami, Florida, on June 6? (26° latitude)
> New York, N.Y., on December 21? (40° latitude)

The answers are 5.5 divided by 1.38, which is 3.9 feet, in Seattle on April 21; 5.5 divided by 14.3, which is .4 feet or about 5 inches, in Miami on June 6; 5.5 divided by .5, which is 11 feet, on December 21 in New York.

The Empire State Building which is 1250 feet, not counting the TV shaft, would throw a shadow on December 21 of 1250 feet divided by .5 or 2500 feet which is very nearly half a mile.

Practice using this table and map and you will have a lot of fun calculating the heights of objects as well as lengths of shadows at various times and different places. Be sure to correct for daylight-saving time in the summer. Solar noon occurs at 1 P.M. daylight-saving time.

LATITUDE

	26°	28°	30°	32°	34°	36°	38°	40°	42°	44°	46°		
Dec 20–31	.87	.81	.75	.70	.65	.60	.55	.51	.47	.43	.38		11–20
Jan 1–10	.90	.84	.78	.73	.67	.62	.58	.53	.49	.44	.40	Dec	1–10
11–20	.93	.87	.81	.75	.70	.65	.60	.55	.51	.47	.43		21–30
21–31	1.03	.97	.90	.84	.78	.73	.67	.62	.58	.53	.49		11–20
Feb 1–10	1.11	1.03	.97	.90	.84	.78	.73	.67	.62	.58	.53	Nov	1–10
11–20	1.23	1.15	1.07	1.00	.93	.87	.81	.75	.70	.65	.60		21–31
21–28	1.43	1.33	1.23	1.15	1.07	1.00	.93	.87	.81	.75	.70		11–20
Mar 1–10	1.66	1.54	1.43	1.33	1.23	1.15	1.07	1.00	.93	.87	.81	Oct	1–10
11–20	1.88	1.73	1.60	1.48	1.38	1.28	1.19	1.11	1.03	.97	.90		21–30
21–31	2.25	2.05	1.88	1.73	1.60	1.48	1.38	1.28	1.19	1.11	1.03		11–20
Apr 1–10	2.74	2.48	2.25	2.05	1.88	1.73	1.60	1.48	1.38	1.28	1.19	Sept	1–10
11–20	3.49	3.08	2.74	2.48	2.25	2.05	1.88	1.73	1.60	1.48	1.38		21–31
21–30	4.33	3.73	3.27	2.90	2.60	2.36	2.14	1.96	1.80	1.66	1.54		11–20
May 1–10	5.67	4.70	4.01	3.49	3.08	2.74	2.48	2.25	2.05	1.88	1.73	Aug	1–10
11–20	8.14	6.31	5.14	4.33	3.73	3.27	2.90	2.60	2.36	2.14	1.96		21–31
21–31	11.40	8.14	6.31	5.14	4.33	3.73	3.27	2.90	2.60	2.36	2.14		11–20
June 1–10	14.30	9.51	7.12	5.67	4.70	4.01	3.49	3.08	2.74	2.48	2.25	July	1–10
11–20	19.10	11.40	8.14	6.31	5.14	4.33	3.73	3.27	2.90	2.60	2.36	June	20–30

MAKING A DATE INDICATOR

You can make yourself a nice date indicator from this table by using the table in *reverse*. Just nail two pieces of wood at right angles to each other as shown in the drawing. The upright piece should be 3 inches high and the long piece can be any length from 10 inches to 15 inches. Now just mark off on the long piece dis-

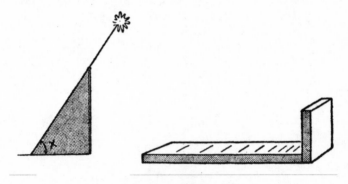

FIGURE 70A

tances from the upright piece according to the dates in the table at the latitude of your home. Just go right down the latitude column dividing 3 inches (the height of your upright shadow piece) by the numbers for each 10 days of each month. Mark off the months on the long horizontal piece and place this shadow stick in the sun. Every day at noon it will give you the date.

Figure 70B shows a date stick marked off for the latitude of New York City. It was designed by dividing all the numbers in the 40°-latitude column into 3 inches—the height of the shadow stick.

13. Here is the way to make an excellent sundial that will keep good time on sunny days. The first thing to do is to determine the latitude of the place you live. Having done that, draw a straight horizontal line and lay off this latitude (the angle φ) by drawing the right triangle shown in Figure 71A. Now draw two circles, one

with the base of the triangle as a radius and the other with the hypotenuse as a radius. Draw a vertical line through the center of these circles and divide the vertical diameter of the smaller circle into five equal parts. Now, count down three of these divisions and

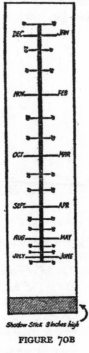

Shadow Stick 3 inches high

FIGURE 70B

draw the horizontal line *DE* as shown in Figure 71 B. Divide the arc *DE* into 12 equal parts and connect each part with the point *O*. Through each division draw horizontal lines parallel to *DE* and, from the intersection of the radial lines with the smaller circle, draw vertical lines forming a series of small right triangles as shown. All these lines must be done in light pencil so they may be easily erased. Now, from the point *O* draw lines that pass

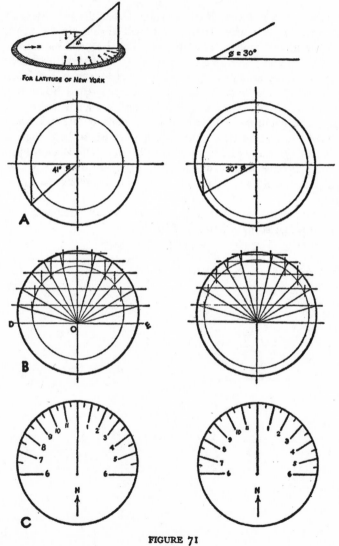

FOR LATITUDE OF NEW YORK

FIGURE 71

through each of these right angles and intersect the circumference of the large circle. These twelve marks will be your number points on the finished sundial. The horizontal line *DE* will now become the 6 A.M. and 6 P.M. line and the twelve marks you just made by the twelve lines passing through the right angles and intersecting the large circumference will be the progressive hours, 7, 8, 9, 10, etc., all the way round the dial. The noon line is the vertical line. The figure shows the finished dial divided into half hours and if you place a right triangular marker whose base angle is the latitude of the place you live on this noon line as shown you have a finished sundial which will keep good time. Be sure to point the noon line to the north when you place the dial in the sun.

To the right of the diagrams *A*, *B* and *C* we see another sundial which is figured for a latitude of 30°.

MATHEMATICAL FALLACIES
AND PROBLEMS

1. Our very first problem·is one of simple multiplication. Let us take any two numbers + fractions and multiply them together. Then let us take the same two numbers + the equivalent decimals and multiply them again. Naturally you would expect the two answers to be the same. But let's see:

$16\frac{1}{2}$	16.5
$12\frac{1}{2}$	12.5
32	8.25
16	33.0
$8\frac{1}{4}$ (half of $16\frac{1}{2}$)	165
$6\frac{1}{4}$ (half of $12\frac{1}{2}$)	·Answer: 206.25
Answer: $206\frac{1}{2}$	

What has happened to the other $\frac{1}{4}$?

2. What is the value of this fraction when $x = 1$? ·

$$\frac{x^2 - 1}{x - 1}$$

Since $x^2 - 1 = 0$ when $x = 1$, and so also does $x - 1 = 0$, we have $\frac{0}{0}$, which is quite meaningless.

3. This is a very old one but it is nevertheless puzzling. Figure 72A shows 64 squares in the big square, that measures 8×8. You. can see how this big square can be cut up and rearranged to form the oblong, which is 5×13 and therefore contains 65 squares. How did that extra square get there?

4. Two wheels are screwed together (Figure 73A). The large wheel is 10 feet in diameter and the small one is 5 feet in diameter.

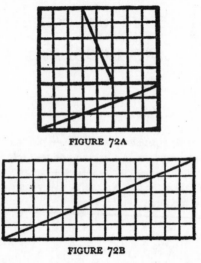

FIGURE 72A

FIGURE 72B

The big wheel rolls on the ground while the little wheel rolls on an elevated platform 2½ feet above the ground. Now it is clear that in one complete revolution of the big wheel it moves through 10 times π feet or 31.41 feet. But so does the little wheel, in spite of the fact that its diameter is only 5 feet and one revolution should move it only 15.70 feet. What's wrong, if anything?

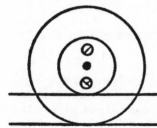

FIGURE 73A

5. Believe it or not, no matter how fast an express train is moving forward, at least a small percentage of it is moving backward. To explain this, consider a car wheel. As you know, it has a flange and part of the wheel is below the rail as shown in Figure 73B. Now it is clear that, as the part of the wheel in contact with the rail is rotating rapidly, the part that comes below the rail is rotat-

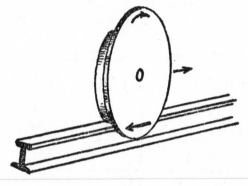

FIGURE 73B

ing just as rapidly in the *opposite* direction. Since this is true for every wheel on the entire train, including the engine, you can see that a certain and definite part of a train moving forward is actually and always moving backward.

6. Sometimes little boys who ask too many questions tie their parents into mental knots. Take, for example, the young brat who asked his father (a professor of philosophy) if God could do anything. Of course the father said "Yes." "Then can he make a stone so large that he can't roll it?" asked junior. The professor was about to say "Yes" again but remained silent.

7. Along the same line of logic as the last item is the barber who shaves everyone in his town who does not shave himself. The big question is: does he shave himself? If he does he is breaking the rule, for he is shaving someone who shaves himself. If he does not

shave himself he is still breaking the rule, for he is failing to shave someone in the town who does not shave himself.

8. A particularly curious problem is the following, each step of which is seemingly true although the result is obviously false:

$$\sqrt{a} \times \sqrt{b} = \sqrt{ab} \text{ (which is correct)}$$

then $\sqrt{-1} \times \sqrt{-1} = \sqrt{(-1) \times (-1)}$ (which is also correct)

therefore $(\sqrt{-1})^2 = \sqrt{1}$.

or $-1 = +1$

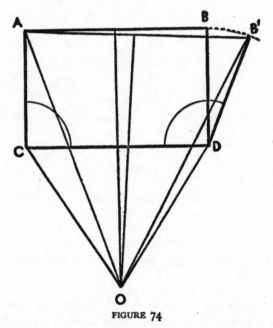

FIGURE 74

9. Here is a remarkable proof that a right angle is greater than 90°. In Figure 74 we see a rectangle $ABCD$ and of course the angles are all right angles. With D as a center and a radius equal to DB draw DB'. Then the angle $B'DC$ is greater than 90°. Now join AB' and erect perpendicular bisectors on AB and AB'. Since

these two lines are neither parallel nor coincident the two perpendiculars will meet in some point O. Now join AO, CO, DO and $B'O$.

The triangles ACO and $B'DO$ are congruent because:

$\qquad AO = OB'$ (it is on the perpendicular bisector of AB')

$\qquad OC = OD$ (it is on the perpendicular bisector of CD)

and $AC = DB'$ ($AC = BD$ and we made BD equal to $B'D$)

The two triangles are congruent (three sides of one = three sides of the other)

Therefore angle $ACO = B'DO$ (same parts of congruent triangles)

But angle DCO = angle CDO (base angles of the isosceles triangle OCD)

Hence angle ACD = angle $B'DC$, or a right angle equals an angle greater than 90° which, of course, is impossible.

What is wrong with this?

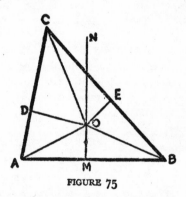

FIGURE 75

10. Every triangle is an isosceles triangle. Take any triangle, as ABC in Figure 75. Draw a perpendicular bisector MN on AB. Now bisect the angle C and extend the bisector to meet the line MN in O. Now draw OD and OE, perpendicular to AC and CB respectively. Join AO and OB.

In triangles COD and COE:

Angle DCO = angle OCE (we made them equal since C is bisected)

The angles at D and E are right angles and the side CO is common to both triangles

CD is therefore equal to CE (same parts of congruent triangles)

Since O is on the perpendicular bisector of AB, $OA = OB$

Since triangles COD and COE are congruent, $DO = OE$

But $AO = OB$, and the angles D and E are right angles

Triangles AOD and EOB are therefore congruent (two sides and an angle are equal)

$AD = EB$ (same parts of congruent triangles)

But we have proved that $DC = CE$

$$\text{and } AD = EB$$

Therefore $AC = CB$, and the triangle is isosceles.

What is wrong?

THE FALLACIES EXPLAINED

EVERY DIFFICULTY in mathematics has an explanation. If it didn't, the mathematicians would be in trouble, for their science wouldn't be exact!

1. This fallacy depends upon the fact that in the first case we did not use the correct rules of multiplication. If we write $16\frac{1}{2}$ as $16+\frac{1}{2}$, and $12\frac{1}{2}$ as $12+\frac{1}{2}$, we then have to multiply four ways and add in order to find the correct answer:

$$
\begin{array}{r}
16 + \tfrac{1}{2} \\
12 + \tfrac{1}{2} \\
\hline
32 \ (16 \times 12) \\
16 \\
6 \ (\tfrac{1}{2} \times 12) \\
8 \ (\tfrac{1}{2} \times 16) \\
\tfrac{1}{4} \ (\tfrac{1}{2} \times \tfrac{1}{2}) \\
\hline
206\tfrac{1}{4}
\end{array}
$$

2. The value of $\dfrac{x^3 - 1}{x - 1}$ *is* actually meaningless when $x = 1$.

This phenomenon is known as a *singular point*, and can be very annoying.

3. If you were to take a piece of graph paper and cut the figures out you would see that in the oblong the four-sided pieces do not exactly fit on top of the triangular pieces. By pretending that they do fit, we enlarge the oblong and make room for the sixty-fifth square.

4. This problem falls apart when we remember that we assumed (incorrectly) that both wheels roll without slipping on both platforms. If the platforms do not move, one wheel or the other will always have to slip during each revolution, by an amount equal to the difference of their circumferences.

5. This is not really a problem. It is a fact that the bottom of the flange moves backward, although it is not what we would expect before thinking about the matter. This helps to explain Dilemma 4, because if we were to place a second rail just touching the bottom of the flange the flange would have to slip on this rail.

6. If you know the correct answer to this problem, you are better than the philosophers, because they have been arguing this question (and many others like it) for thousands of years. This dilemma shows why philosophy is not yet an exact science.

7. This is another famous dilemma in philosophy. It is the same in principle as: "Lawyers never tell the truth. I am a lawyer." If I am a lawyer, I am not telling the truth, and therefore I am not a lawyer. If I am not a lawyer then I *am* telling the truth, and I am a lawyer! To explain these and other paradoxes, Bertrand Russell devised his "theory of types," which holds that statements involve particular "universes of discourse," beyond which it is risky to apply them.

8. To reach this result, we must fail to take account of the fact that $\sqrt{1}$ is either $+1$ or -1, since the square root of any positive number is either positive or negative. In this problem, we have to take the negative root, or -1, to keep the algebra correct. The positive square root, $+1$, is called an *extraneous root*, because it pops up where it doesn't belong.

9. The origin of this fallacy is difficult to find. The error is in

the diagram. If properly constructed, the point O is so far down that the line OB' is actually on the other side of the point D; when the diagram is properly drawn, the theorem cannot be proved.

10. If this were true, it would upset all of our ideas of geometry. The fallacy is again hidden in the diagram. The point O actually lies *outside* the triangle, and either perpendicular OD or OE (but not both) falls outside of the triangle. Again, if we draw the diagram correctly, the theorem cannot be proved, and the rules of geometry are still as good as they ever were.

THE CIRCLE SQUARED AND THE
ANGLE TRISECTED—OR ARE THEY?

ALONG WITH the trisection of an angle with a straightedge and a compass, and in the same impossible category mathematically, goes the construction of a square that shall be equal in area to that of a given circle.

Mathematicians have proved that it is impossible actually to square the circle with a ruler and a compass because π is irrational, which means that its value is not a simple fraction but a decimal that continues forever.

In addition to being irrational, π is also transcendental, which means that it is not the solution of an algebraic equation. In this way it is quite different from $\sqrt{2}$ or $\sqrt{3}$. Square roots, while irrational, are easy to represent by lines. An isosceles right triangle whose sides are 1 actually does have a hypotenuse that is $\sqrt{2}$ and here we have a straight line that represents an irrational number, namely $\sqrt{2}$. This proves that we can show by means of straight lines, values of square roots (all of which are irrational!) and these values are geometrically accurate and theoretically perfect because of the famous Pythagorean theorem.

But the value of π is another matter. If it could be shown to a great degree of accuracy by a straight line we could use this straight line as the side of a square or rectangle and easily construct the square which will be equal in area to that of a given circle. From a purely practical standpoint there is nothing to prevent us from doing this because of a certain remarkable fraction. If you divide 355 by 113 you will get 3.14159292 which differs from π by less than three ten-millionths. No instrument devised by man could ever detect the difference between this 3.14159292 and the true value of π which is 3.14159265 . . . If we were to determine the circumference of the earth by this value of π and then use the true value of π our error would be only 14 feet in nearly 25,000 miles!

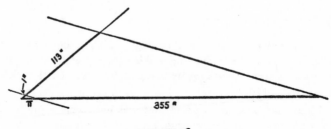

FIGURE 76

To construct this amazing value of π geometrically and with practically perfect accuracy, we lay off on a very long roll of paper a line that shall be exactly 355 inches long (29 feet 7 inches) and, using a dividing line at any angle at all, lay off exactly 113 inches (9 feet 5 inches). If both lines are *exactly* these lengths, not a fraction of an inch more or less, and their ends connected (Figure 76), a line parallel to that connecting line through the 1 inch mark on the dividing line will mark off 1/113 of 355 inches or exactly 3.1415929 . . . inches on the long line. For all practical purposes we can call this division π.

If we now take this as one side of a rectangle and R^2 as the other side, the area of the rectangle will be $πR^2$, which will certainly equal the area of a circle of radius R. This is shown in Figure 77. The area of the rectangle agrees with the area of the circle (where $R = 2$) to an accuracy of 1 in 9,000,000. To appreciate how incredibly accurate this is, let us examine the difference in two circles whose radii are 1 mile each. In the first circle we use the true value of π; in the second circle we use this value 355/113. We get:

$$\pi \times 5280^2 = 87582584.46092 \text{ square feet}$$
$$355/113 \times 5280^2 = 87582576.53376 \text{ square feet}$$

Here we see a difference of less than 8 square feet in more than 87,000,000. Surely, from a practical standpoint, we have squared the circle since no instrument could possibly find any error in our work.

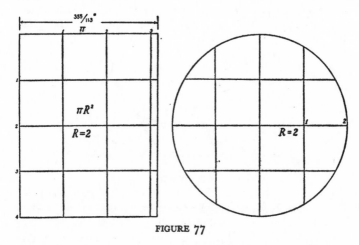

FIGURE 77

Well then, have we or haven't we squared the circle? From the standpoint of the practical man, the surveyor or engineer, we have done a magnificent job of approximately squaring the circle with an accuracy far greater than anyone or any machine can detect. But from the standpoint of the mathematician we have *not* squared the circle and we never will. Mathematics is an *exact* science where a statement is either right or wrong (or meaningless as in the case of zero divided by zero). There is no such thing in mathematics as "almost true." This amazing value of π, which is far more accurate than necessary to the practical bridge designer, civil engineer or surveyor, is just as wrong as $2 + 2 = 5$ to the mathematician who can prove conclusively that no line ever drawn can equal the true value of π.

Now that we have, for all practical purposes, squared the circle, let us do the other impossible job of trisecting an angle. There is a great misconception in this so-called impossible mathematical feat. Nothing is much easier than trisecting an angle with a ruler and a compass yet nothing is more impossible than trisecting an angle with an *unmarked straightedge* (therein lies the difference) and a compass. Here is the way to trisect any angle and prove it:

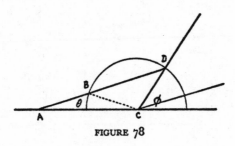

FIGURE 78

In Figure 78 we see the angle ϕ which we wish to trisect. With C as a center draw any semicircle cutting the base line. Now take a straightedge and *mark off* the radius of this semicircle on it. Call the length of this radius AB. Now lay this straightedge in such a manner that it touches the intersection of the semicircle with the side of the angle (point D), the point B touches the semicircle and the point A is on the base line as shown in Figure 78. This makes an angle θ with the base line and this angle is just one third of angle ϕ.

The proof of this trisection is extremely simple: Since $BC = AB$,

ABC is isosceles and θ = angle *BCA*. But angle *DBC* is twice angle θ. Now simply draw a line through *C* parallel to the line *AD*. Obviously the smaller angle equals θ and the larger angle equals angle *DBC*. But angle *DBC* = 2 angle θ, consequently angle ϕ equals 2 times angle θ + angle θ, or 3 times angle θ.

INTERESTING PROBLEMS THAT
REQUIRE SOME THOUGHT

(Answers on pp. 171-74)

1. Can you make 1000, using only eight 8's?
2. Can you make 100, using only four 7's?
3. Can you make 20, using only two 3's?

In the problems given above, you must use only the numbers mentioned and no others. You may use any process in arithmetic to solve the problems. To illustrate: in order to make 100 with four 9's we could write 99 9/9 or to make 5 with three 5's we could write 5/5 × 5.

4. A man had eight half dollars, one of which was known to be a counterfeit and slightly heavier than the rest. Assuming that the man had a good pair of scales, how can he find the bad half dollar in only *two* weighings?

5. If the number $A B C D E \times 4$ equals $E D C B A$, what different numbers (zero being excluded) do these five letters represent?

6. A grocer has a scale and four weights. If nothing in his store weighs more than 40 pounds and these four weights enable him to weigh every single pound from 1 to 40, how much does each weight weigh?

7. If $\frac{PORK}{CHOP} = C$, and C is greater than 2, what different numbers do *PORK* and *CHOP* represent? None of the letters stands for zero.

8. A man bought a watch for $103, including the tax. He paid for it in eight bills, but they were not five twenties and three ones, and there were no one-dollar bills among the eight. How did he pay for the watch?

9. What is the smallest number in which the digits are reversed when 2 is added to its double?

10. In chess a queen can move as many squares as she chooses diagonally, horizontally or vertically.

FIGURE 79

As you know, a queen can capture a queen, if it is on a square in its path. Now, can you place 8 queens on a chess board so that no queen can capture any other queen?

11. A young man was once asked his age. He replied as follows: "My grandfather was sixty-five when I was born. Gramp's age when he died this year, on his birthday, was the square root of the year in which he was born added to the square root of a recent presidential election year." How old is this obnoxious young man?

12. If a steel band were stretched tight around the earth at the equator so that it touched it everywhere, how much would the band have to be increased in length if it were placed one foot off the earth all the way around? Assume that the earth is level at the equator.

13. I have two children who are not twins. The cube of my son's age added to the square of my daughter's age gives the year in which my wife was born, which event occurred in the nineteenth

167

century. If I am five years older than my wife, how old are we all in 1952?

14. A group of women bought a number of items at a bargain counter. All of the items sold for the same price and the total amount paid by all the women was $2.03, exclusive of the tax. If each item cost more than 10¢, how many women were in the group and what did each item cost?

15. Twice a fraction plus half that fraction times that fraction equals that fraction. What is the fraction?

16. A piece of typewriter paper 8½″ × 11″ is folded as shown in the diagram. As you can see, the angle that the top of the paper makes with the left margin is 45° and the projection AB is 2 7/8″. What is the length, to one-tenth of an inch, of the fold CD?

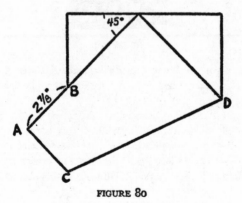

FIGURE 80

17. My son's age is the same as my father's with the digits reversed. The product of their ages gives the recent year in which my son was married. If I am twice as old as my son, how old am I, how old is my son, and how old is my father?

18. A railroad runs straight from Punkton to Junkville. Mainfield is on this line just half the way between Punkton and Junkville. Hotberg is just as far from Punkton as it is from Mainfield

and Mainfield is as far from Hotberg as it is from Junkville. If it is twenty miles from Punkton to Hotberg, how far is Hotberg from Junkville?

19. A man is the same age as his wife with the digits reversed. One eleventh of the sum of their ages equals the difference in their ages. How old are they? Assume the man to be older.

20. What are the areas of the narrow and the wide rectangles from the information given in the diagram?

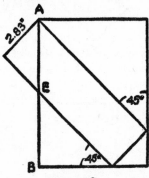

FIGURE 81

21. During the Second World War, General Nuisance, in an order of the day, issued the following statement:

"This was a bad day for Nippon. The number of Japanese prisoners taken in the present drive can be easily found from the following simple addition:

$$\begin{array}{r} NIPS \\ QUIT \\ \hline QUICK \end{array}$$

To help you along I'll tell you that $S = 5$, $P = 4$, $T = 3$ and N is not 1." How many Japanese prisoners did General Nuisance take?

22. A carpenter had to construct a table 2 ft. square from the odd-shaped board shown in the diagram. He did it in two sawings and wants to know if you can do the same.

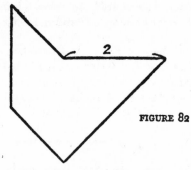

FIGURE 82

23. Can you transform the square shown below into five small equal squares whose total area shall be equal to the square, with only four cuts?

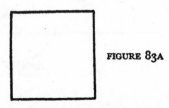

FIGURE 83A

24. If you ·can solve this innocent-looking problem in plane geometry, you are better than many mathematics teachers. Try it and see how far you can get.

Given: Triangle *ABC*. *BE* = *CD* and the angles *B* and *C* are bisected.

To prove: Triangle *ABC* is isosceles.

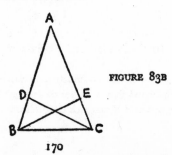

FIGURE 83B

The proof is extremely long and far too involved to go into here. Take it to your mathematics professor and let him struggle with it.

ANSWERS

1. $8 + 8 + 8 + 88 + 888 = 1000$
2. $7/.7 \times 7/.7 = 100$ or $77/.77 = 100$
3. $3!/.3 = 20$ (remember that 3! signifies $1 \times 2 \times 3$)
4. He divides the group into three parts of three, three and two. He then weighs the three against the three. If they balance, the bad coin is one of the remaining two, which another weighing will quickly reveal. If they do not balance, he weighs two of the group of three that was heavier on the first weighing. If these two balance, the bad coin is the one left out. If they do not balance, the bad coin is the heavier of the two.
5. The numbers are $21978 \times 4 = 87912$. A can't be 1, since $4 \times E$ must equal A, and E would then have to be a fraction. A can't be 3 or more, since the product would then have to have more than 5 places. Hence A must be 2. If A is 2, we have the question: 4 times what ends in 2? Hence E might be either 3 or 8. But E can't be 3, since $4 \times A = E$, and we know that A is 2. E must therefore be 8. We then have:

$$
\begin{array}{r}
2 \ . \ . \ . \ 8 \\
4 \\
\hline
8 \ . \ . \ . \ 2
\end{array}
$$

We know that $4 \times B$ can't have a "carry-over," or it would spoil the 8 which we know E is. B can't be 2, since A is 2, and it can't be more than 2 since it would have a "carry-over" when multiplied by 4. B must therefore be 1. Now $4 \times D$ must end in 1; after taking account of the "carry-over" of 3 from the 4×8 ("put down 2 and carry 3"), we see that D must be 7, and the rest is easy.
6. The weights are 3^0, 3^1, 3^2 and 3^3 or 1, 3, 9 and 27 lbs. These four weights by addition and subtraction will weigh every pound from 1 to 40 inclusive.
7. C is greater than 2, and it can't be 4 or more, since $C \times CHOP$ would make more than four places. C must be 3, and P is therefore

9. Since C times *CHOP* equals *PORK*, K must end in 7 since 3×9 equals 27. K is therefore 7. We then have:

$$\frac{9 \; . \; . \; 7}{3 \; . \; . \; 9} = 3$$

C times H cannot have any "carry-over," since that would spoil the 9 which we know P is. The only number that H can be is 2. Now $3 \times H$ must give us O. O can't be 1, 2, 3, 7 or 9; it is either 4, 5, 6 or 8. By testing 4, 5 and 6 we find that they do not fill the bill. Hence O must be 8 and the answer is:

$$\frac{9 \; 8 \; 6 \; 7}{3 \; 2 \; 8 \; 9} = 3$$

8. One fifty, two twenties, a five and four twos.

9. 25; $(2 \times 25) + 2 = 52$.

10.

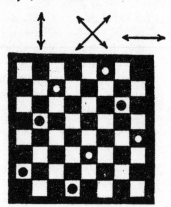

FIGURE 84

11. Only two recent years have simple square roots: 1849, whose square root is 43, and 1936, whose square root is 44. The sum of these roots is 87 which was gramp's age when he died. The young man is $87 - 65$ or 22.

12. It would be $2\pi r \times 1$ or 6.28 feet longer—no more and no less than would be added to the circumference of a sphere of any size if 1 foot were added to its radius.

13. My son can't be 13 or more since the cube of his age would be 2197 and we are still in the twentieth century. He can't be 10 or 11 since the cube of his age would give a figure which, when added to the square of my daughter's age, would require my wife to be born far too long ago to permit her to have so young a son. My son, therefore, must be 12, whose cube is 1728. The only possible age for my daughter is 13 since 13^2 is 169 and this, added to 1728 gives us 1897. If my daughter was 14, my wife would have been born in 1924, outside the nineteenth century. She could not be 12 or she would be a twin. If she was 11, my wife's birth would be pushed back to the impossible date of 1849. Hence, in 1952, I am 60, my wife is 55, my son 12 and my daughter 13.

14. There must be 7 women, each paying 29¢. This is because there are no numbers, other than 7 and 29, that will make 203 and since the price of each article is more than 10¢, there cannot have been 29 women, each buying a 7¢ article.

15. The fraction is 2/5. Reduce this to tenths and we have:

$$.8 + .2 \times .4 = .4$$

16. The length of *CD* is 9.2 inches.

17. Trial and error for this one. A fairly recent year must be in the 1940's or 1950's. In this recent year my son was married, so it is possible that he was then in his early twenties and my father in his sixties. This condition suggests 26 and 62 but their product is 1612 and surely my son was not married then. So my father might be in his seventies. Try 27 and 72. This gives 1944 when multiplied, and is the only possible solution. I must be 54.

18. Since Hotberg is equidistant from Punkton and Mainfield, and since Mainfield is also equidistant from all the towns, Hotberg, Punkton and Mainfield make an equilateral triangle, whose angles are therefore 60°.

But this makes the triangle joining Hotberg, Junkville and Mainfield isosceles. Since the angle of this triangle at Mainfield is 120° (180°·—60°), the other angles must be 30° each.

But this makes the triangle joining Hotberg, Punkton and Junkville a right triangle, with its right angle at Hotberg. With the hypotenuse 40 miles and one side 20 miles the other side must be $\sqrt{(40)^2 - (20)^2}$, or about 34.6 miles.

19. His wife is 45 and he is 54. The sum is 99 and difference is 9.

20. The large rectangle is 48 square inches; the small one is 24 square inches.

21. If S is 5, P is 4, T is 3 and N is not 1, we have to start with:

```
. . 4 5
. . . 3
───────
. . 8
```

By inspection, N must be 9 and Q must be 1, making V 0, so we have:

```
  9 . 4 5
 1 0 . 3
─────────
1 0 . 8
```

I cannot be anything but 2, and the problem is completed. The General took 10,268 prisoners.

22.

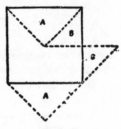

FIGURE 85

23.

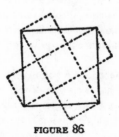

FIGURE 86

Table of Logarithms

1—100

N	log	N	log	N	log	N	log	N	log
1	0. 00 000	21	1. 32 222	41	1. 61 278	61	1. 78 533	81	1. 90 849
2	0. 30 103	22	1. 34 242	42	1. 62 325	62	1. 79 239	82	1. 91 381
3	0. 47 712	23	1. 36 173	43	1. 63 347	63	1. 79 934	83	1. 91 908
4	0. 60 206	24	1. 38 021	44	1. 64 345	64	1. 80 618	84	1. 92 428
5	0. 69 897	25	1. 39 794	45	1. 65 321	65	1. 81 291	85	1. 92 942
6	0. 77 815	26	1. 41 497	46	1. 66 276	66	1. 81 954	86	1. 93 450
7	0. 84 510	27	1. 43 136	47	1. 67 210	67	1. 82 607	87	1. 93 952
8	0. 90 309	28	1. 44 716	48	1. 68 124	68	1. 83 251	88	1. 94 448
9	0. 95 424	29	1. 46 240	49	1. 69 020	69	1. 83 885	89	1. 94 939
10	1. 00 000	30	1. 47 712	50	1. 69 897	70	1. 84 510	90	1. 95 424
11	1. 04 139	31	1. 49 136	51	1. 70 757	71	1. 85 126	91	1. 95 904
12	1. 07 918	32	1. 50 515	52	1. 71 600	72	1. 85 733	92	1. 96 379
13	1. 11 394	33	1. 51 851	53	1. 72 428	73	1. 86 332	93	1. 96 848
14	1. 14 613	34	1. 53 148	54	1. 73 239	74	1. 86 923	94	1. 97 313
15	1. 17 609	35	1. 54 407	55	1. 74 036	75	1. 87 506	95	1. 97 772
16	1. 20 412	36	1. 55 630	56	1. 74 819	76	1. 88 081	96	1. 98 227
17	1. 23 045	37	1. 56 820	57	1. 75 587	77	1. 88 649	97	1. 98 677
18	1. 25 527	38	1. 57 978	58	1. 76 343	78	1. 89 209	98	1. 99 123
19	1. 27 875	39	1. 59 106	59	1. 77 085	79	1. 89 763	99	1. 99 564
20	1. 30 103	40	1. 60 206	60	1. 77 815	80	1. 90 309	100	2. 00 000
N	log	N	log	N	log	N	log	N	log

FIGURE 87

$$y = \log_a v$$

$$y + \Delta y = \log_a (v + \Delta v)$$

$$\Delta y = \log_a (v + \Delta v) - \log v$$

$$= \log_a \left(\frac{v + \Delta v}{v} \right) = \log_a \left(1 + \frac{\Delta v}{v} \right)$$

$$\frac{\Delta y}{\Delta v} = \frac{1}{\Delta v} \log_a \left(1 + \frac{\Delta v}{v} \right)$$

$$= \log_a \left(1 + \frac{\Delta v}{v} \right)^{\frac{1}{\Delta v}}$$

$$\frac{dy}{dv} = \frac{1}{v} \log_a e$$

FIGURE 88